10.95

MEMBER
OF THE
LEGISLATURE

Acknowledgements

The author and publisher wish to express their thanks for the following: to *The Toronto Star* for cartoons by Franklin, Macpherson, Pilsworth and Fons von Woerkom, to *The Globe and Mail* for cartoons by Franklin and Reidford, to *The Toronto Sun* for cartoons by Donato, to *The Windsor Star* for cartoons by Roschkov and Donato. The cartoon by the late Al Beaton originally appeared in *The Toronto Telegram*.

MEMBER OF THE LEGISLATURE

Morton Shulman

Fitzhenry & Whiteside

Toronto Montreal Winnipeg Vancouver

© Fitzhenry & Whiteside Limited 1979

Fitzhenry & Whiteside Limited
150 Lesmill Road
Don Mills, Ontario M3B 2T5

Canadian Cataloguing in Publication Data

Shulman, Morton, 1925—
  Member of the Legislature

ISBN 0-88902-417-0

1. Shulman, Morton, 1925— 2. Legislators –
Ontario – Biography. I. Title.

FC3076.1.S58A3   328'.713'0924   C79-094153-8
F1058.S58A3

Printed in Canada

Contents

Preface

I was appointed Chief Coroner of Metropolitan Toronto
in 1963 by Premier John Robarts. For four stormy years
I fought the Conservative provincial government, the
municipal authorities, federal departments and the medical profession over reforms I attempted to make in a
dozen different fields. I scored a number of notable vic-
tories resulting in major changes in highway construction,
boating regulations and hospital operation procedures.
But my superiors couldn't stand me or the constant adverse publicity I generated and in March 1967 my career
as Coroner came to a sudden end.

The final blow-up took place over the burning down
of a "fire proof" government hospital and my insistence
on going ahead with an unwelcome inquest into a death
in that fire. Attorney General Arthur Wishart ordered
me to back off. When I did not he summarily fired me.
I went out in a blaze of publicity, charges and counter-
charges.

Uncertain of the effect of all this controversy upon the
public, Premier Robarts put off the provincial election
until the fall, appointed a Royal Commission to investigate my charges, and sat back to wait it out. From my
point of view the obvious place to continue the battle
was on the political war field. My problem was that I

was a Tory, had been appointed Chief Coroner as an act of Conservative political patronage, had been asked to run as a Tory candidate on several occasions, and had no connection with either of the other parties. Now it was clear that I would have to jump to one of them.

Their courtship began immediately. The Liberal party was then headed by Bob Nixon, a decent, intelligent, highly principled man from a farm background in Western Ontario. Nixon had succeeded to the leadership of the party largely by default, as others abandoned the post either through illness or attraction to richer Liberal rewards in Ottawa. His essential decency actually turned out to be a liability in provincial politics, for his courtesy and gentility never did appeal to the mass of Ontario's voters. And his refusal to stick in the knife when the situation demanded it often left the field open to the more aggressive New Democratic party.

Two days after I was fired Nixon called me and asked if we could meet. I visited him in his suite at the Royal York Hotel where he invited me to run as a Liberal candidate, hinting broadly that I would receive a cabinet post if he formed the government. I was mightily impressed and would probably have jumped at the offer, but at the very same time that I was talking to Bob Nixon his deputy, Elmer Sopha, was making a speech in the Ontario legislature saying that the Tories were right to have fired me. This aroused my doubts and those doubts were strengthened when, at a second meeting, Bob Nixon confided that some wealthy Liberal backers didn't want me and had threatened to cut off donations if I joined his team. But he insisted that he still wanted me and that he was the boss, and soon afterwards I was approached by a federal Liberal MP who offered me $100,000 in campaign funds if I would declare for the provincial Liberals.

As my Liberal courtship simmered, I was approached by the NDP, but instead of summoning me, Leader Don-

" I'M THINKING OF PLACING MY FIGHTING ABILITIES AT YOUR DISPOSAL . "

ald MacDonald and his deputies, Jim Renwick and
Stephen Lewis, came to my home where they shrewdly
took the high road. There was no talk of money or
socialist philosophy; instead they spoke of the good
work I had done as Chief Coroner and offered me a
forum to continue that work. They appeared as pure as
the angels, with a total lack of self-interest, and they said
I could run in any riding in the province. Stephen Lewis
even offered to vacate his own seat if I wanted to run
there.

I was mightily impressed but still held back because I
was and am an unrepentant capitalist (the author of a
book called *Anyone Can Make a Million*) and a believer
in free enterprise. Moreover, I had observed only too

well how socialism in power in England had weakened that country's economy.

On the other hand, with only eight seats in the 117 member Legislature I obviously did not have to worry about the NDP coming to power. And Donald MacDonald was a most appealing leader, brilliant, incisive and dogged, he combined Nixon's decency with an aggressive instinct that had nursed the NDP from near oblivion to a point where both the old major parties were concerned about its growth.

My hesitations were finally settled by the Tory government. John Robarts called an election for October and meanwhile his Royal Commission, headed by a former Tory official, was giving me a "royal" roasting. I obviously needed allies and the numerous but weak Liberals offered me no help. Stephen Lewis, however, sent his father, David Lewis, to talk down my tormentors at the Royal Commission and this settled my doubts. I joined the NDP.

As soon as I joined, some of the NDP window-dressing fell away. They dropped their promise of "any" riding and quickly shoved me into High Park, an area of West Toronto heavily populated with eastern European voters, where the NDP consistently ran a poor third. The party leaders correctly foresaw that I would easily win that area, where I had been born and where I carried on my medical practice, and they hoped that an overflow effect would help them break into the surrounding area where they did not hold a single seat.

As for me, I was so anxious to get at the Tory enemy that I didn't argue or particularly care where I ran. I was so full of anger that I didn't really question my new friends and I suspect they used me rather easily. When I was fired I had been working on a number of terribly important projects, one involving organ transplants in medical research and another investigating the causes of auto deaths. I told the public, and myself, that I wanted to get into politics to continue my work. But looking back now I think that at the time I was so mad at being fired that plain ordinary fury was the main reason I ran. I wanted to be a member of the Legislature and face my adversaries on their own territory.

1 *The Beginning*

There is no experience in the world quite like being a
member of the Legislature: tremendous prestige with the
bureaucracy, initials after your name, special licence
plates, passes to railways, airplanes and the CNE, cut-rate
hotel rooms, cheap liquor at any hour at Queen's Park,
the press hanging on your words, the less privileged
petitioning you for favours or just for your presence at
their banquets. It is a heady experience that gives the
illusion, if not the reality, of power. Oddly, no one has
ever before written the story of what it's like to be an
MPP.

On October 17, 1967, I was elected as the NDP member
of the Ontario Legislature from High Park. It wasn't
much of a contest. The sitting Conservative member was
a pleasant but colourless representative who had not become well known even in his own riding and I rode into
office on a flood of publicity produced by my work as
Chief Coroner and subsequent firing. The election itself
was a breeze. I swamped the opposition with an army of
over a thousand volunteers and we were so successful in
our saturation tactics that I scored almost exactly double
the vote of the sitting member. There was also the fact
that people don't vote against their doctor; and my
medical office sat in the dead centre of the riding. In

1

fact, in the immediate area of my office I won an incredible 75 per cent of the vote.

I had joined the NDP less out of concern for their policies than in reaction to what I saw as the sins of the Tories and the weakness of the Liberals. And my hasty embracement of the socialists would inevitably lead later to some ludicrous situations. I had little knowledge of what the NDP stood for and I am equally sure that the leaders of the party, in their anxiety to make short term gains, gave little thought to the embarrassment of clasping a wealthy and unregenerate capitalist to their bosom.

In any case, I was now an MPP. And I found to my amazement that I had absolutely nothing to do. As Chief Coroner I had dozens of cases to work on at all times and I had to select which ones to give my time. Now, after fighting an exciting election campaign, suddenly everything stopped. The Tories had been re-elected with a reduced majority, the Liberals were still the official opposition and the NDP had jumped from eight to twenty seats but were still the third party. The government was satisfied with the situation and Premier Robarts was in no hurry to call the Legislature into session.

The day after the election I went down to the Parliament Buildings but no one paid me the slightest attention. When I complained, I was assigned the use of a secretary for one day a week and was given a desk in the huge NDP secretaries' office. But my request for a phone and a private office were met with hoots of laughter. I quickly learned that an MPP in 1967 was a party appendage – meant to show up and vote the appropriate way on suitable occasions and expected to draw his pay and hold his tongue the rest of the time. It was all very anticlimactic.

I had made only two campaign promises. I had, first of all, promised the disabled and impoverished occupants of Runnymede Hospital that, if elected, I would see that they received a disabled person's allowance. (Some of them were so poor that they couldn't even afford to buy shaving cream or writing paper.) Secondly, I had gone through the riding (or rather my wife, Gloria, had – I never did get enough nerve to knock on a stranger's door to ask him to vote for me but fortunately she had no such inhibitions) promising that, if elected, I would eliminate the stench pervading High Park from the Canada Packers' and Swift's packing plants. By a stroke of great good luck, Swift's plant burned down the day after the election. Then, to my amazement, the president of Canada Packers called me to his office to announce that his firm was installing pollution control equipment.

I didn't have the slightest idea of how to get a disabled person's allowance enacted. While awaiting the opening of the Legislature, where I intended to politely ask the government to enact this change, I looked about for something else to do. A reporter friend suggested, "Why don't you advertise? Ask people who have beefs to write you. Try auto insurance. Everyone's mad at the insurance companies." It sounded like a great idea and I promptly placed ads in the *Globe and Mail* and the *Toronto Star* asking "persons who have been unfairly treated by auto insurance companies" to write to me. Immediately my enforced leisure ceased. By return mail, hundreds of letters poured into Queen's Park – the result of many years of mistreatment of their policyholders by the auto insurance companies. The heavy-handed response of the insurance companies brought further publicity. One of the companies actually ran an ad in response announcing the compilation of a file of "persons who believe that certain political parties should remain out of the automobile business."

I was delighted and promptly released a few of the worst cases to the press – obvious injustices like the case of the man who had an $80 accident and had his insurance charges promptly raised by $80 per year; or the case of the woman whose car was damaged by a falling branch but whose company refused to pay on the grounds that the branch had fallen from the weight of ice and her policy excluded ice damage. The papers gave this considerable space and the government ministers responsible were mightily annoyed.

At last, Premier Robarts announced that the House would open February 14. I could hardly wait to take my first shot at the government. What I didn't know was that there was equal anticipation and confidence on the ministers' benches.

2 *The Shot Heard around Queen's Park*

The public is under the illusion that an MP or MPP can bring things up in the House at will. In actual fact, however, ordinary members are given only two chances a year to speak to the Legislature on matters of their choice. And even then there is not sufficient time allotted for every member to get his two chances. (Fortunately, many government backbenchers choose not to speak at all.) As a result of this inability to voice matters of concern to himself and his constituents, the MPP is constantly seeking ways around the rules. One of the most common ploys is to raise a matter in the House in the form of a question.

When I first entered the Legislature a member could ask unlimited numbers of questions provided that he gave the minister concerned a copy of the question some hours in advance and that the question involved a matter of urgent public importance. The Speaker of the House, former Attorney General Fred Cass, ruled his department with an iron hand. And his decisions on what was of "urgent public importance" inevitably led to bitter quarrels with unhappy backbenchers whose questions he disallowed. To complicate matters, Mr. Cass in his wisdom had ruled that no question could begin with the word "why" which led to strange convolutions of the

English language as the members struggled to get information without using that essential word. (I could not even ask him "why" he had made that ruling.)

The Legislature began each day with Question Period: an hourly circus in which the opposition members hurled questions at the ministers not so much for the purpose of getting information as to embarrass a minister or to get personal publicity. In reply, the government spokesman responded with a minimum of facts and a maximum of pointing out the incompetence of the opposition. Question Period was then, and it still remains, the high point of the legislative day. As soon as it is over and the House moves on to bills or speeches, it is amazing to see how quickly both the members and the press depart. There is a rule that twenty members must remain in the House to maintain a quorum, but, when I first arrived, there was a gentleman's agreement that no one would ask for a quorum call so that often there would be only ten or twelve members sitting there, with some of them fast asleep. I soon managed to change that!

February 15, 1968 came around, the first day of regular business of the Legislature, and I was determined to begin my campaign against the Tories with some newsworthy attack on one of them. I decided to start at the top by striking a blow at a long-time Canadian Conservative tycoon, E.P. Taylor, and directed my first question to the deceptively mild-looking Provincial Secretary, Robert Welch. "Is the government prepared to prosecute E.P. Taylor and the directors of Canadian Breweries for their refusal to hold annual meetings of Peller Brewing Company, a public company as per section 306 of the Corporations Act?"

I could not have chosen a worse minister to tangle with. Bob Welch has a disconcerting resemblance to Mr. Peepers, but this masks a sharp mind and an exceptional ability to crush an opponent while appearing to be helpful. He shook his head across the House at me in apparent bewilderment. "I don't understand what you mean. Taylor is not a Peller director so why should we prosecute him? And if the Peller company has not been holding annual meetings why should Canadian Breweries be prosecuted?"

Welch appeared to be asking me a question but Fred Cass gave me no chance to reply to it. Under the rules, opposition members could ask questions but never give answers so I couldn't tell the House (and the press) that Taylor controlled Canadian Breweries and that company in turn controlled Peller's. Instead I was forced to sink to my seat in absolute embarrassment while the Tory benches rocked with laughter and satisfaction. The much heralded white knight newly arrived in the opposition benches was going to be easy to handle! (Although Bob Welch demolished me in the Legislature, his executive assistant made a phone call that afternoon. A few weeks later Peller's Brewery held their first annual meeting in fourteen years. In fact, they held fifteen annual meetings that same afternoon to cover all the annual meetings missed back to 1954!)

I quickly learned two lessons from this trouncing. First of all one had to carefully pick which ministers to attack. Although many of them were sitting ducks, others, like Welch and Bill Davis (whom I shall discuss later), should be avoided at all costs. The other lesson was that it was foolish to expect either sympathy or further investigation from the press gallery. Only if they smelled blood would they act, springing instantly to the side of the winner. It was essential, therefore, to get *all* the facts into the wording of the question, preferably in a way that suggested the minister was either incompetent or ignorant.

Attorney General Arthur Wishart proved an unexpectedly easy foe and over the next few weeks I peppered him with a series of embarrassing questions relating to the Coroner's Office. My first chance came only four days after my initial disaster in the House. A thirty-nine-year-old man had gone to the Queensway Hospital with chest pain, had been sent away as medically fit, and had dropped dead twenty minutes later. I demanded that a post-mortem and inquest be held, but the Attorney General strangely ruled that such an investigation should not take place. The next day the *Toronto Star* front-paged the story of the man's widow, telling of her shock that her husband's death could be so casually dismissed. The

coroner on the case did not help the Attorney General any with his statement that "The public must learn that such things are possible, in fact, common . . ." Despite all the publicity, there was still no investigation of the matter.

Economics Minister Stanley Randall and Health Minister Matthew Dymond proved equally easy targets. An internal survey of Randall's department had described poor employee morale and one of my patients had shown me a copy of the survey. When I asked the minister what he was doing about it he sputtered in fury; and when I asked Matt Dymond about a minor disturbance at one of the hundred-odd hospitals under his jurisdiction he foolishly (and honestly) replied, "I don't know what he's talking about." The Tory backbenchers no longer laughed when I rose. Instead they roared with anger and attempted to drown me out with heckling. I loved it!

It was all small potatoes for the government. But it got me publicity. And this brought me to the notice of the legion of unhappy bureaucrats who work at middling positions for the Ontario government and who hate their bosses. Gradually my mail began to contain more and more plain brown envelopes containing secret reports and documents detailing government mismanagement. These dictated the subsequent course of my political career.

3 The Tories and My Bank Manager

An amazing mix of people began to send me information about wrongdoing.

- A switchboard operator at stock broker Rennie & Company had listened in to the conversations of her boss with the president of Shell Oil and heard the oil executive tell the broker that his company was going to take over the Canadian Oil Company (then trading at $40) at $55 per share. The broker made $5 million for himself and his oil executive friend by using the credit of Rennie. When this information later began to leak out, a letter was made up and predated which purported to show that the oil executive was taking the financial risk. After the broker submitted this letter to the Securities Commission he realized that it proved he had the advance knowledge of the takeover that he had earlier denied. As a lesser evil he admitted that the letter was a fake. The head of the Securities Commission had written to the Attorney General suggesting that criminal charges be laid but nothing was done.
- One of my former coroners had discovered that, through a mixup at the morgue, two bodies had been interchanged and a post-mortem report on one of them had been assigned to the other. An amazed and disturbed

widow had asked Supervising Coroner H.B. Cotnam how her husband could have gained sixty-six pounds and two inches and had been reassured that this was due to "post-mortem changes."

• The unhappy deputy governor of the Don Jail told me the amazing story of how the crooked president of Northern Ontario Natural Gas had been sprung out of jail three and a half years earlier. He had submitted X-rays purporting to show that he was dying of cancer but which were in fact his brother's X-rays. Following his release he had returned dramatically to good health. At that time the man had served a mere four months and Attorney General Arthur Wishart had said that "further charges would not be proceeded with so long as he is in his serious state of health."

• The honorary consul for Peru brought me the incredible story of how the Catholic Children's Aid had been exporting Canadian babies to Peru for adoption with the full knowledge of Ontario's Department of Social and Family Services.

• The proprietor of a boarding home for the mentally ill had complained publicly that the $3 per day fee per patient was insufficient to properly care for the sick. This was followed by the immediate removal of all patients from her home.

• Dozens of letters came from workers who felt they had been mistreated by the Workmen's Compensation Board. Some of the stories sounded as if they had come straight out of Charles Dickens: for example, the horribly scarred fire victim who was offered total compensation of $30 for his scars.

• Coroner Dr. John Porter called to tell me that the department's research study of traffic deaths had been summarily cancelled despite the Attorney General's assurances to the contrary in the Legislature.

I thought all these stories had the makings of a major

scandal and proceeded to make the error of detailing all of them in a three day long blockbuster speech which began March 4. It was all too much for the press, who find it difficult to focus on more than one issue at a time. Although they reported my speech, none of the scandals were followed up. The government didn't even bother denying my charges but just let them lie there and be gradually forgotten. I learned another important lesson from this: never give the press more than one story at a time. They just don't have the space or the energy to get excited over more than one thing per day.

My speech did have an exciting ending. Frustrated beyond words, ambitious Tory backbencher Eric Winkler jumped to his feet as I sat down. Completely forgetting the government's decision to ignore me he charged that I had a "very sadistic political mind" and demanded that I explain: (First) "The ugly circumstances in which I replaced Smirle Lawson as Chief Coroner of Metro." (Second) "A bank manager who came under the machination of the honourable member for High Park." (Third) "The financial losses of a druggist in Peterborough."

Winkler was as new to the Legislature as I and did not know that a member cannot make charges about another without substantiating evidence. As soon as he had completed his remarks, both the NDP and the Liberals demanded that he either substantiate or retract his comments. In the hubbub that followed the House was reduced to chaos. The Speaker finally called for an adjournment, with the understanding that the next morning Winkler either had to provide more proof or else retract.

I awaited the next day's session with some anxiety. I had often told the story of how John Robarts had made a political deal with me to appoint me Chief Coroner in return for my engineering the Tory nomination for one Cass Bielski in the Parkdale riding of Toronto. And I wasn't at all upset by the story of the Peterborough druggist who had lost money in the stock options business (he was in competition with a firm in which I was a partner and I had nothing to do with his losses) for it had all been fully detailed in the press. But what was the story about my bank manager? I barely knew the man and had no idea what Winkler was going to say about him.

I am told that the Tories held frantic meetings later that night with Eric Winkler as they struggled for a way to extricate themselves from this mess without any more embarrassment than necessary. The next morning, Winkler rose to document his charges. He said that on two occasions I had admitted being appointed Chief Coroner as a result of political patronage. He then read comments made by Chief Justice Gale in his judgement in the stock options case in which my stock partner, Wilf Posluns, had sued the Toronto Stock Exchange. "Unquestionably Dr. Shulman is blessed with a brilliant and facile mind. However, his performance as a witness probably suffered because of being so endowed, for at times he responded so quickly as to invite the notion that he was too glib to be entirely truthful. On occasions he certainly contradicted himself perhaps for that very reason, or perhaps he did not stop to consider his answers before making them, and I came to the conclusion that where his evidence was found to be in conflict with that of a calm but reflecting witness, I should accept that of the latter."

And that was it. Incredulously I asked Winkler, "What about my bank manager?" and he replied, "I made no reference to the honourable gentleman's bank manager – none."

And so ended my first battle in Queen's Park. Confused and inconclusive, it was the forerunner of many more serious fights to come. The *Globe* summed it up, "It is always surprising to realize that there actually are people who believe the most effective weapon against fire is fire. Adherence to this theory may be the explanation for the astonishing performance at Queen's Park when Conservative Eric Winkler fired back a round of verbal buckshot at Dr. Morton Shulman . . . The Conservatives may be hardpressed to handle this prickly young upstart but they surely must realize now that bombast isn't the answer. Bombast is Dr. Shulman's game."

The *Star* wrote, ". . . Eric Winkler, Conservative MPP for Grey South, seems to have clinched the prize for the silliest parliamentary speech of 1968."

4 *The Jails*

One of the privileges granted to MPPs is that of visiting provincial institutions, including reformatories and jails, and speaking to the inmates. From the mass of letters I had suddenly begun receiving from prisoners, I suspected that something had gone wrong in Ontario's prisons. I decided to tour the province to see for myself. I asked respected lawyer, philosopher and fellow NDP member Patrick Lawlor to accompany me because I was afraid that if I reported abuses on my own the Tories would neither listen to me nor believe me. Beginning in March of 1968 we travelled to a different institution every weekend for a year and made some startling discoveries. Among them:

• Toronto's Don Jail had a large cage in which prisoners referred by the courts for a mental examination were kept for weeks on end, guarded by "orderlies" selected from the convicted drunks currently in jail. There was absolutely nothing for the caged prisoners to do or read and the so-called "mental examinations" were done by the jail doctor – a general practitioner observing the patients' behaviour for a few minutes through the bars.
• At the Mercer Reformatory for women we found a notice prominently displayed stating that inmates would

not be eligible for parole if further charges were pending against them. Despite this, millionaire mining promoter Viola McMillan, who was serving time for "wash trading" (selling stocks on the exchange to and from yourself to give the illusion of public interest in the stock) and had charges of fraud pending against her, had been paroled the very day the notice was posted.

• A mental defective had been erroneously labelled as mentally okay and sent to a reformatory.

• Wages in the provincial institutions for working prisoners had been set at six cents per day up to a maximum of $20, and no prisoner left a reformatory with more than that sum. In contrast, the federal prisons paid 35 to 80 cents a day and savings were encouraged.

• At the Guelph "reformatory" only ten per cent of the prisoners were receiving vocational training that would lead to a job after release.

• Unruly prisoners were disciplined at Guelph by forcing them to "run the gauntlet": two lines of guards with clubs who beat them as they ran. The most recent incident had resulted in two men suffering a concussion, and two others lacerations that required stitches.

• Guards at all the jails had been instructed to write down verbatim and report back to head office immediately all conversations Lawlor and I had with any inmate or guard.

The Department of Reform Institutions was a long neglected branch of the Ontario government, a ministry which had always been considered the dumping ground for incompetent ministers or for those about to retire. Prisoners don't vote and no one at Queen's Park gave a thought to the jails. Indeed, all that was expected of the ministry was a minimum of expense and no fuss. Shortly before Pat Lawlor and I were elected, a new minister had been appointed in the person of Allan Grossman. He was radically different from his predecessors in his desire to modernize and improve the institutions in his care. Unfortunately he was also a very thin-skinned politician, highly intolerant of criticism, and he responded to our charges in the Legislature by denying everything, charging that we were troublemakers, and on one occasion stalking from the House in fury. He counter-attacked vigorously and suggested our visits and questions were impairing security in the prisons and were, in fact, helping to produce riots. Grossman did very well with this technique for a while but he got caught when he denied the use of beatings in runnings of the gauntlet at Guelph, since it later turned out that several inmates had been hurt badly enough to be taken to a doctor. As Ron Haggart put it in the *Telegram*, "It had taken three weeks to establish the facts. Why didn't Allan Grossman, Minister of Reform Institutions, just tell the truth the first time?"

The minister finally got the point. Over the next two years the gauntlet was abolished; Guelph Reformatory was reduced sufficiently in size so that all occupants received vocational training; persons referred for a mental exam actually received one; and a rapid program of jail modernization was instituted.

Perhaps it all would have happened anyway. But I believe we hurried it along.

5 *Matthew Dymond*

The Minister of Health at that time was Matthew Dymond, a small town general practitioner who had apparently been given his portfolio because he was the only doctor on the government benches. He proved to be well-meaning but quite out of his depth. And we were soon at each other's throats.

The trouble all began when Mrs. Janet Gurman, proprietor of a nursing home in Collingwood, appealed to me for help when the Department of Health suddenly notified her that the patients in her home were to be removed and her nursing licence cancelled. Officials of the department refused to give either Mrs. Gurman or myself reason for this action and went ahead to forcibly remove her weeping patients.

On April 28, 1968 I told the story to the Legislature and demanded an explanation. The Minister of Health refused to explain. This led to a tremendous uproar in the House, with both the Liberals and the NDP demanding an answer. The minister was finally saved when the House Leader, Leslie Rowntree, adjourned the proceedings.

When the House sat the next day Dr. Dymond presented a horrendous story of beatings and abuse of the patients by Mrs. Gurman. He said that according to the sworn evidence of nursing home employees Mrs. Gurman had physically beaten many elderly patients, had forced one patient to drink her own urine, had diverted patients' food to the staff, and had misused sedatives and tranquillizers. The other MPPs believed the Health Minister and when he concluded by saying that the evidence was being turned over to the Attorney General so that criminal charges could be laid, Dr. Dymond received prolonged applause from both the Conservatives and the Liberal opposition. Eric Winkler summed the matter up by accusing me of "sensationalism" and "political expediency." And that's where it rested.

Even the press accepted Dr. Dymond's story at face value. As the *Globe* put it, "Dr. Shulman takes a position rather compulsively without bothering to examine all the facts on a situation and once he has formed his opinion he is intolerant of any other position and of anyone who holds it."

But not one detail in Dr. Dymond's story was true. There had been sixteen nurses and nurse's aides working in that nursing home. Within days I had sworn statements from fifteen of them stating that they had never seen any patient abused. It turned out that Dr. Dymond's speech and the behaviour of his department had been predicated on a letter received from a nurse who had been discharged from the home. The government had little choice at this point, however. They proceeded to lay charges against Mrs. Gurman – which, under rules of the Legislature, prevented any further debate.

One year later Mrs. Gurman was found not guilty. But by that time she had lost her property and her business, for which losses she would never receive a cent of compensation.

This terrible case had taken its toll on Dr. Dymond and he began making errors which the press picked up and magnified. Thus, a few days later I asked him why his department did not distribute measles vaccine along with their other serums and he blurted back, "How would I possibly know?"

This was followed by the Health Minister going on an economy binge at Ontario's hospitals for the mentally ill. Patients had been encouraged to work in the hospitals' laundry, dining room and farm grounds by paying them a nominal five cents an hour which they could use for sweets or cigarettes. When I revealed that Dr. Dymond was cutting this grandiose sum to two cents an hour, the government was greatly embarrassed and the Premier furious.

The next battle took place in December after Lakeshore MPP Pat Lawlor and I visited the Smiths Falls Home for the Retarded. As we were taken around this terribly overcrowded hospital we heard a litany of misery, culminating in one of the supervisors giving us an example of the shrunken and shredded uniforms given to the patients. When we returned to Queen's Park and displayed the clothing, demanding an investigation, Dr. Dymond responded by ordering the OPP to investigate and lay charges against the staff member who had "stolen" the clothing to give to us. And to prevent further scandals coming out he issued instructions that MPPs were to be barred in the future from making unannounced visits to his institutions.

The final showdown with the Health Minister took place when a staff psychiatrist at the Brockville Hospital came to me with a story of neglect of patients, understaffing, theft of drugs, and toleration of sexual intercourse between patients and staff. Dr. Dymond indignantly denied everything and the House set up a committee to investigate.

While their investigation droned on I short-circuited Dr. Dymond's ban on hospital visits by hiring a firm of detectives at my own expense. They placed operatives as orderlies in several Ontario mental institutions and these worthies fed me a continued series of mini-scandals over the next few months.

It was all too much for Dr. Dymond who decided to

pack it in. He cited his "heavy workload" and gave the Premier his resignation. The Toronto *Telegram* gave the doctor a fine eulogy and said that he quit because of my harassment. In a way I was sorry to lose him. He had been such an easy target.

6 *How I Harassed a Poor Widow*

Some of the other ministers were not as soft as Dymond. Treasurer Charles McNaughton was particularly adept at political rough-and-tumble and it didn't take him long to make a fool of me. In my mail in March of 1968 was a letter from one Phil Glanzer who described himself as a "small bill collector" and who accused the Treasurer of refusing to enforce a garnishee order issued by the courts against one of the employees in the Treasurer's office. Glanzer enclosed a copy of the court order. The next day in Question Period I made the mistake of asking McNaughton why he was flouting the court.

When the minister replied he really dished it out. It turned out the employee in question was a widow with four children whose husband had just died of leukemia and who was struggling to pay off the medical bills. McNaughton demanded to know what my association with the bill collector was and he accused me of harassing the poor widow. He finished up by saying that he would continue to protect the poor widows of this world against the likes of Glanzer and myself!

Boy – did I feel like Simon Legree! The Tories made the most of my blunder and the story appeared in every newspaper in the province.

Actually, although McNaughton was very effective in debate in the Legislature, he turned out to be a dis-

astrous Treasurer. Though he was bright, he was quite
an innocent in financial matters. On July 4, 1968 he announced that Ontario intended to borrow some hundreds
of millions of dollars from West Germany in order to
save one per cent in interest charges. I tried in vain to
reason with him. It was common knowledge that Germany intended to revalue the mark. I said to the Treasurer, "You may save one per cent in interest but when
the time comes to pay it back, you may lose infinitely
more."

McNaughton refused to listen, replying that "the
possibility of revaluation in Germany is very unlikely."
He proceeded with the German loan.

It is odd that the press never picked this up for that
decision was one of the most disastrous financial moves
Ontario ever made. The mark was revalued upwards
again and again over the next eight years and the Treasurer's loans ended up costing the province an extra
$150,000,000. Charles McNaughton didn't stay around
to reap the results of his folly. He retired and was re-
warded by a grateful province with an appointment as
Chairman of the Ontario Racing Commission.

James Auld was another minister I never got the
better of. Auld's department was then responsible for
film censorship. At a party I had heard Magistrate Dave
Coons describe how he had attended a meeting of senior
Ontario civil servants, where the entertainment had been
a pornographic film supplied by the censor board. For
many years the censor had collected and assembled in
one super pornographic extravaganza the better tidbits
excised from films too raunchy for the rest of us to see.
To titillate senior Tories this unusual montage was shown
to them on special occasions. I questioned Auld about
this in the House. My problem was that I had sworn not
to name my source and Auld defended his department
by flatly denying that the event ever took place. Once
again I had egg on my face.

I did a little better when the censor blundered and banned a film called *The Titicut Follies*. I suspect that the film was banned on the basis of its title and that it had never been screened, because in actuality it was a documentary on the treatment of the mentally ill in Massachussetts. I managed to borrow a copy of the film from the U.S. distributor and showed it to the press, meanwhile challenging Jimmy Auld to charge me for breaking the law. Although I won that round in publicity terms, the ban never was lifted. It is very difficult for any government to admit that it has made a mistake.

7 *Sleeping MPPs*

All of these simultaneous battles with the various ministers took place in the archaic atmosphere of the Legislature; a place where members showed decorum and respect by wearing jackets and ties regardless of the heat, but where it was quite proper to put up one's feet and sleep through the debates.

Part of the problem was my doing. As I have said, the rules of the Legislature require a quorum of twenty members, but there had been a gentleman's agreement to ignore this, and sometimes the number present would drop to as low as ten or twelve members. So long as the Speaker was not forced to take official notice of the shortage of members nothing was done. But I found a delightful way to harass the government by periodically rising and demanding a quorum. The bells would ring and the members would all be summoned to the chamber thinking a vote had been called.

The Tories responded to this nuisance by rotating the requirement that their members be present in the House. They would take their time in shifts, come in and go to sleep. One evening I viewed the impressive sight of elderly and fat Tory backbenchers, Ellis Morningstar and Norris Whitney, sound asleep, feet on their desks, heads dropped back and mouths wide open. It was too much – I slipped out, got my camera and snapped a picture.

One of the non-sleeping Tories saw me point the camera. He jumped to his feet and alerted the Speaker who ordered the Sergeant-at-Arms to seize my camera. He did grab it but before he got to me I passed the film to my seatmate, Fred Young. The furious Tories demanded that I be punished for this gross breach of etiquette, but the Speaker couldn't quite figure out what punishment to mete out and the matter was dropped.

Not, however, before the enraged Conservatives vented their spleen. Allan Grossman called my behaviour "disgraceful and despicable." Charles McNaughton roared, "he has given evidence of how despicable he really is," and James Auld got in the best line: "He can't see a belt without hitting below it." I'm afraid I infuriated them all even more when I announced that I intended to use the picture to illustrate a new book called *The Decline and Fall of the Conservative Party.*

It turned out that I wasn't a very good photographer. When the film came back from the developer it was too blurry for use. But I had made my point – no one slept in the House after that night.

The Tories gave in equally easily when I took off my jacket one sweltering summer day. At first they threatened to expel me. But, realising how foolish they would look in the press, they quickly yielded on this old rule. I wish that the more important wars were as easily won.

Some of these House skirmishes had important consequences, at least for those immediately involved. The NDP members tended to be sober and puritanical but the government members, and some of their Liberal opposition, had the bad habit of indulging to excess before night sessions – which they attended in a frankly drunken condition. There is nothing more irritating than attempting to discuss a constituency problem with a minister so drunk he can't understand what you are saying. And I finally lost my temper one night with Les Rowntree, the Minister of Financial and Commercial Affairs, and called to the Speaker, "The Minister is drunk."

There was bloody hell to pay. I had broken a "gentleman's rule" again and for this I was completely ostracized and thoroughly hated by the Tories. The papers gave it a huge play and shortly thereafter Rowntree resigned from the cabinet and left politics.

But I never again saw a minister enter the House under the influence.

8 *Sneaking into INCO*

I had entered politics as the darling of the press as a result of my stint as Chief Coroner. But the honeymoon ended at once when I announced for the NDP. I became the target of open hostility. I still received vast publicity for my crusades and capers, for this helped to sell papers, but I was no longer reported fully, or even factually, while my opponents were given the royal treatment. Editorial writers turned hostile across the province. (There were two exceptions: the *Globe and Mail* remained fair and the Kingston *Whig Standard* continued to support me.)

It actually reached the point where a reporter from the Toronto *Telegram*, who approached me for my assistance in writing a full-page profile of myself, prefaced his request by saying, "I've been ordered to do a hatchet job on you but I'll try to be fair." The story duly appeared as a hatchet job, filled with inaccuracies and outright misstatements of facts, and I rather foolishly replied with a personal attack on the *Telegram*'s publisher, John Bassett, in the Legislature. I had not yet learned not to fight with journalists – let alone publishers. The *Telegram*, of course, had the last word, riding me mercilessly until it folded. At one point in reporting one of my speeches, it actually reached the point of saying that I was "snarling in the House."

I got into trouble with the *Toronto Star* in an odd way. Complaints had been coming out of Sudbury for years that pollution within the huge INCO plant was far in excess of government standards, but that every time inspectors were due to arrive from Toronto, INCO knew about the visit in advance and would clean up. To find out the truth, the *Star* sent reporter Marc Starowicz to Sudbury where, at considerable risk to himself, he climbed during the night over the massive slag heap that dominated the rear of the complex. Starowicz discovered that all the rumours about excessive sulphur dioxide were true and returned to Toronto where he submitted his story to the *Star*. Starowicz's supervisor was delighted; he congratulated him on his fine work and submitted the story for publication. But from the upper levels of the paper, instructions came down that the story was to be killed. Three months later, a disaffected *Star* employee (not Starowicz) gave me a copy of the Starowicz story and I read it in the House, thanking the *Star* for doing the research.

Publisher Beland Honderich was furious and a confused Starowicz was summoned from assignment in Montreal for a dressing down from editor Martin Goodman. The reporter who actually leaked the story to me was never detected and subsequently went to work for a rival outlet. (I was mightily amused some years later to hear Goodman innocently attempting to lure him back.) The enmity of the *Star* towards me never died. Ten years later, when they started up their Sunday edition and I was suggested to Beland Honderich as a possible columnist, he is reported to have replied, "The pole has not been cut long enough with which I would touch Morton Shulman."

The INCO story had a fascinating ending for me. The local union invited me to come to Sudbury to see for myself and so on January 23, 1969, with a three-day beard, fatigue jacket, dungaries and a borrowed worker's badge, I walked into INCO with the night shift and spent eight hours measuring SO$_2$ levels. The safe reading for SO$_2$ is a maximum of five parts per million and my gauge showed that the actual level was over 200 parts per million, the top reading on the gauge. The smell, the heat and the humidity were unbearable – it was indeed like Dante's inferno. I came back to Toronto and told my story in the Legislature and to the press. Mines Minister Allan Lawrence reacted immediately by ordering government inspectors to stop giving INCO advance notice of their visits.

I'm not sure if that turned out to be a victory or a defeat since INCO solved their in-plant pollution problem by pumping more of the SO$_2$ into the outside atmosphere!

9 *The Workmen's Compensation Board*

The Workmen's Compensation Board (WCB) has come a long way in the past ten years and, looking back now, it is hard to believe just how cruelly we used to behave towards injured workers.

A typical injustice of the period involved a man of 45 who had injured his back at work but who was refused full compensation because his X-rays showed some degenerative arthritis. The board must have been aware that almost everyone over thirty shows such changes but they persisted in cutting the payments, on the grounds that without the arthritis the accident would not have produced such bad results. Similarly, heavy labourers who hurt their backs and who, after a time, were half better would have their compensation cut in half even though they were still unable to return to work.

The WCB was very tough on formalities and if the injured worker didn't report the accident at once, or if he didn't have a witness, the case would be routinely turned down.

Also many firms found they could save money by not reporting minor injuries to this board. If some of these minor cases later turned serious the company would solve its problems by firing the worker.

The case that brought the situation at the wcb to a head was that of Rose Szego who developed asthma after working in a fur factory for some years. Mrs. Szego had a mound of medical evidence which proved that her asthma had been produced as a result of exposure to the furs. But the wcb turned down her claim on the grounds that there had been "no accident." Mrs. Szego applied to legal aid for help in appealing to the board but that body refused to help her because "the case could not be won."

On October 31, 1968 I took Mrs. Szego's appeal to the wcb. I told them that if they turned her down I intended to relate the details in the Legislature and then to go across the province with the story of their coldness and indifference. The board gave in on Mrs. Szego. After I won her case, I raised several dozen other cases of obvious wcb injustice in the Legislature, and this publicity produced too much heat for the government. The wcb suddenly reversed their entire policy on the back and other injuries about which in the past they had been adamant. Bruce Legge, the board's chairman, was made the goat and forced to resign, even though he had merely been loyally carrying out the policy set out by the Tory government. Of all the battles I had with the Conservatives, this victory had the greatest effect on the most people. I'm very proud of it.

Legge's place was taken by Mike Starr, an old Tory politician, who proceeded to carry out the new liberalised rules. Oddly enough, labour was neither mollified nor grateful and complaints against the new board are even more numerous (although usually less justified) than were those against the old.

10 *All Speeches Shall Be Sung in Tune*

It bothered me that I had not been able to carry out my pre-election promise to provide a government comfort allowance to impoverished patients in hospitals for the chronically disabled. Although I had on several occasions raised the matter with John Yaremko, Minister of Social and Family Services, he had refused to budge. Finally I got an idea and in March 1969 sent a letter to the residents of the tiny Runnymede hospital in my riding telling them of my efforts and of Yaremko's refusal to go along. I sent a copy of the letter to the minister with the promise that the same letter would go to the many thousands of chronically disabled persons across the province in just ninety days.

It worked instantly. The minister saw the light and just twenty-five days later he brought in the required order in council. Sometimes blackmail works!

Before I entered the Legislature, Question Period had not been exploited and rarely lasted longer than a few minutes. But I had soon realised that this was an easy place to embarrass the government and began asking questions daily: at first one or two, then five or six and finally fifteen or twenty in a single day. I was copied quickly by other NDP members, then by the Liberals, and finally even by a few backbench Conservatives (with friendly planted questions) and the daily Question Period began eating up an hour or more of the House's time. Fred Cass was under steady pressure and gradually backed away from his tough stance, allowing almost every question to be asked. He felt that it was up to the government to do something. Finally, Premier Robarts called a meeting of the three party heads and a compromise was worked out. From then on members could ask questions without prior notice and could also ask supplementaries to questions asked by other members, but Question Period was to be limited to 45 minutes daily.

It was a pyrrhic victory. The rules stated that backbenchers were limited to one question but the two leaders, Nixon and MacDonald (soon to be replaced by Stephen Lewis), could ask unlimited questions before the backbenchers were given any time. The leaders selfishly exploited their opportunity and would use up anywhere from twenty to forty minutes of the Question Period every day. To my utter frustration I found that I now had to battle with forty other backbenchers for the opportunity to get in a single question.

This situation persisted for five years until the NDP became the official opposition and Bob Nixon was replaced by Stuart Smith. Smith and Lewis finally agreed to limit themselves to three questions each, but by this time I was out of politics.

As for private bills, this was supposedly an opportunity for an ordinary member to bring in a proposed law to be considered by the entire Legislature. In actual fact it was so much window dressing, for the government never allowed these bills to reach a vote. Early on I attempted to force a vote on one of my bills on a day when most of the Tories were away and was ruled out of order by the Speaker. When I persisted, the Premier warned me that if I insisted on a vote he would abolish private members' hour entirely.

Forcing a vote was useless anyway. Every time I called

a snap vote, the Speaker would rule that the Tories had won, even if we outnumbered them two to one. If the opposition demanded that the vote be called individually, the Speaker would ring the bells and not take the count until enough Tories had arrived to give them a majority.

At first I felt that private bills were one way of influencing the government and I brought them in by the score, ranging all the way from highway changes to appointing an ombudsman, to a bill controlling ethics of MPPS. Many of these ultimately were picked up by the government and became law. I am well aware, however, that this was because their time had come and had nothing whatsoever to do with my sponsorship.

Finally, I became convinced that no one was paying any attention to my private bills and, as a test, brought in "an Act to regulate the proceedings of the House" which read as follows:

Her Majesty, by and with the advice and consent of the Legislative Assembly of the Province of Ontario, enacts as follows:

Commencement and rule for House	1. From now until the first of June all speeches shall be sung in tune. The Speaker shall determine which honourable members are in tune.
Supply Committee	2. When in committee of supply, the House may hum, but not too high. The clerk shall choose the key.
Band, playing of	3. A band shall nearly always play except on the first day, behind the Speaker's chair at 3:00 and on the terrace after tea.
When House shall sit	4. The House shall never sit on sunny days unless there is a thick haze. And they shall rise if they have met, when it's foggy, fine or wet.
Cessation of Hansard	5. Except as here and after hinted, Hansard shall not again be printed and save as in this Act is learned all previous Hansards shall be burned.

Procedure for Treasurer	6. The Honourable Treasurer shall now proceed to Rome, to Moscow, Washington, Cathay or anywhere that's far away.
Offence	7. The penalty for each offence shall be elastic but immense.
Application of Act	8. Finally this Act applies and shall be good for anybody who thinks it should, provided that if strong objection shall be expressed to any section, that section shall not have effect except for those who don't object.
Short title	9. This Act may be cited as the *A.P. Herbert Bill to Regulate the Proceedings of the House.*

It was a straight steal from a joke played by a famous English comic in the House of Commons some fifty years ago.

To my no great surprise the bill slipped through and no one noticed it for days!

11 *Victories I Would Regret*

There were two battles which I actually won which, looking back, I wish I had lost: bail reform and medicare. I became involved with bail reform through Robert Sweezie, a twenty-year-old Sudbury youth charged on June 25, 1969 with theft and forgery. Bail was set at $300 which Sweezie couldn't raise and, as a result, he remained in jail for seven months awaiting a court date. When he contacted me in February 1970, no date was yet available due to the heavy court backlog. I bailed the lad out and raised hell. As a result, it emerged that seventeen persons had been held in the Don Jail for four or more months without a final court hearing.

These revelations were followed by a flood of letters from the jails describing similar cases. They all made headlines and resulted in editorials right across the country. Both the Ontario and Federal governments were impressed and the Bail Reform Act ultimately followed, with all its horrors. Actually, I had my initial second thoughts long before when I discovered to my dismay that every one of the individuals whom I had championed and got out of jail were back in trouble and back in jail remarkably quickly. Even Sweezie didn't show up for his trial because he became smashed with hashish! I wish I had never become involved in that issue.

Similarly with medicare. I had fought for government-paid insurance from the beginning. Now I am awed at just how wrong I was and at how impossible it is to solve the problems I (and others) created. Doctors are miserable with the system, patients are short-changed in terms of the doctors' time, the paper work is overwhelming and medical standards have slipped perceptibly. But it's free: and no political party has the guts to tackle the problem. At the rate it is growing it may well bankrupt the country by 1985!

12 *Leaks*

I had now spent two years in the Legislature and my relationship with the Tories had, if anything, deteriorated.
There was a new Health Minister now, Tom Wells, and
instead of rescinding Dr. Dymond's rule forbidding visits
by MPPs to public institutions he had tightened it. In
response I had expanded my "spy" network in government institutions and now had about a dozen civil servants reporting to me on what was going on in their
departments – specifically in relation to waste and
mismanagement.

The government reacted somewhat ineffectively, setting
up a committee of three senior civil servants to seek out
the names of my informants. This committee ordered
that signs be put up in all government offices pointing
out the penalties for breaking their oath of secrecy. But,
despite their efforts, the flow of information continued
– of shortages of drugs, mistreatment of patients, corruption, unsafe buildings and plain inefficiency. The
reason the committee was so unsuccessful was that it
was headed by one Fred Pinder, the director of the
Safety Branch of the Department of Public Works, who
had personally been supplying me with information and
secret reports of terrible mismanagement, waste and
corruption within his own department.

Since they couldn't shut off the flow of information, the Tories and their allies responded with vituperation. The *Telegram* called me "sleazy" and a "McCarthyite" and *Consensus*, the official organ of the Tory party, called me "despicable" and "odious." They said I was synonymous with "deceit, subterfuge and megalomania."

Premier Robarts personally ordered his cabinet to detect any "spies" in their departments. And, in his anxiety to produce results, Works Minister John Simonett, who had been plagued with leaks, fired a hapless and quite innocent inspector, one Sidney Greenslade, whom I had never met. This happened because I had released a copy of a secret report from the Department of Public Works which revealed that fifteen government buildings in Toronto were fire hazards. Greenslade had worked on that report and Simonett concluded erroneously that he was my source.

I rose in the Legislature and swore that Greenslade had never given me any information. But the government wouldn't listen and I failed to save the inspector's job.

The Tories now detested me so thoroughly that they automatically rejected any suggestions I might make. I did not help matters when I printed up 25,000 copies of extracts from Attorney General Arthur Wishart's estimates of November 1969 and mailed them to each of Mr. Wishart's Sault Ste. Marie constituents. This material included speeches by the Attorney General which indicated something less than competence in his position. I suggested that if, after reading them, they felt that "the Minister of Justice would be better suited to another department, please write to the Premier of the province, requesting Mr. Wishart's transfer to a less demanding post." That caper was no success on my part: the Premier received two hundred letters critical of Mr. Wishart and 1,180 supporting him!

The low point of all this bickering came on November 27, 1969 when I had this edifying exchange with Tom

Wells on the subject of 999 Queen Street West, the ancient mental hospital. It was preceded by my demands that something be done about the disgusting conditions in the hospital and I punctuated my speech by holding up in the Legislature blown-up pictures of (1) A row of iron beds covered with thin mattresses, lying side by side, ten inches apart, without even a curtain between them; (2) A row of toilets with no doors; (3) A hundred-year-old bathtub on a wooden platform.

I roared, "The situation is shameful. It's enough to make your blood boil," and Hansard records the following:

Mr. Wells: You have a closed mind.

Mr. Shulman: You have no mind.

Mr. Wells: You practise the big smear and the big lie.

Mr. Lewis: You're a cynical and impossible guy.

I followed up by blasting the hapless Mr. Wells for the staff shortages and mistreatment of inmates at Penetang, the centre for the criminally insane. A sixteen-year-old who had attempted suicide had been transferred there from Guelph Reformatory, where on arrival, the boy was stripped and put in the care of two older prisoners who promptly forced him to indulge in homosexual acts.

Obviously this situation of open war between me and the Health Minister could not go on. Both the government and myself were beginning to look terrible in the press, but the government had more to lose than I did. John Robarts recognized this and, in mid-December he threw in the towel, directing Tom Wells to cancel the order forbidding MPPs access to government institutions. In response, I dismissed the detectives I had placed in the mental institutions.

But I had one more horrible quarrel with Tom Wells just a few days later. It all started with a phone call from Dr. Z. Gorecki, the new medical superintendent of the Cornwall Psychiatric Hospital. Dr. Gorecki was of Polish extraction and upon his appointment to the hospital he had discovered a patient in the ward, one Micholas Gilewicz, who spoke only Polish and who Dr. Gorecki felt was quite sane.

Gilewicz had been picked up by the police ten years earlier for getting drunk and whistling at a priest and, because his conduct and language had appeared strange, he had been transferred to a mental hospital. There, no one could understand what he was talking about. And there he remained for ten years until spoken to by Dr. Gorecki.

I examined Gilewicz' file and found the following entries: (April 1960) "It is impossible to find any evidence of delusional thinking at present." (April 1964) "Has difficulty understanding questions put to him – certified as mentally ill."

And for the next five years there was not a single entry indicating that any doctor ever saw him again.

The government released Gilewicz after I raised a fuss and returned the $14,000 left from his savings after charging him two dollars per day board for his nine years' incarceration. But Tom Wells was unrepentant. In fact, he accused me of misleading the House and produced evidence that Gilewicz was in fact paranoid in 1960. I requested that the case be referred to the Health Committee for investigation to determine who was telling the truth. Instead, Premier John Robarts proposed an investigation before the Committee on Privileges and Elections "to determine how many times a member should be able to use his seat for this sort of allegation."

The Premier didn't follow through on his threat: the government was happy to see the matter blow over in a manner favourable to itself. But, meanwhile, it set up a committee in every mental hospital to check each patient annually and make sure another Gilewicz case could not occur.

Geoffrey Stevens summed up the situation in the *Globe and Mail*:

> To anyone who spends a few days in the public galleries of the Ontario Legislature, it soon becomes apparent that Dr. Morton Shulman – the small man with the harsh voice that fills the chamber, the one playing Hamilton Burger to John Robarts' Perry Mason – has not yet learned to love the Government.
>
> To be fair, it must be admitted the Government is not exactly lovestruck by its erstwhile but very lapsed disciple. Hate is the word that defines their relationship – a blind, uncomprehending sort of hate. Despite more than two years of daily warfare, neither has figured out how to handle – or destroy – the other.

13 *The NDP: Not One Happy Family*

While all this was going on things were not running smoothly within my own party. In early 1970, Stephen Lewis had challenged Donald MacDonald for the leadership of the NDP, resulting in MacDonald's resignation. I felt and said publicly that in my opinion the people of Ontario would never vote for a party led by the brilliant but hawklike Lewis. I suspect that all the NDP MPPs shared that belief but that most of them preferred the irresponsibilities of being in the opposition to the prospect of forming the government, and so they rallied behind Stephen Lewis. Three or four of us tried to stave off his victory by persuading Walter Pitman to run against him. But it was a losing contest and Stephen easily won the leadership convention. I knew then that my political career would not be a lengthy one: Stephen's views and mine on everything from economics to simple justice were further apart than expediency could possibly bridge. From this point on, I gave up attending caucus meetings entirely (I'd always thought they were a waste of time) and for the next four years followed my own course in the Legislature.

I had other political troubles outside Queen's Park. One major problem of the NDP is its total democracy, for it is this very democracy that attracts a great variety of assorted left wing kooks, Marxists and Trotskyites. These individuals are not interested in the NDP per se but rather in finding a platform for themselves and for their ideas – which are normally totally ignored by both press and public. They tend to join weak riding organizations, where they can hope to gain control. And this came awfully close to happening in High Park.

I had been paying little attention to the riding association which for thirty years had meandered along under the aegis of ex-MPP and long-time prohibitionist Bill Temple. I had noticed that a few young and very outspoken new members had worked their way on to the executive. But I didn't realize what was happening until one day I was summoned to an executive meeting for a "self criticism" session! It was something straight out of Red China: my sins at Queen's Park were pointed out, I was told where I had deviated from the party line and was instructed to be more careful in future.

I was lucky. The Marxists had a majority of the executive but they had moved too quickly. Their support in the riding association itself was still a tiny minority and they should have built up their membership before striking at me.

Riding elections were only one month away and Bill Temple cannily let the Marxists appoint two of their members to the three man nomination committee which predictably brought in a slate dominated by themselves. But Temple had done his homework. When election night came, he nominated a second slate from the floor.

The Marxists' defeat was total. And so was their surprise. We cleaned them off the executive and they walked out that night never to be seen again.

14 *Me and the Mafia*

While I was playing these minor political games I became embroiled with organized crime and the Mafia in a way that changed my entire future, and actually led to a $50,000 contract being taken out on my life.

In January 1969 I received an anonymous letter on the stationery of the Ontario Provincial Police saying that if I wished to receive information from the Justice Department and was prepared to treat the source as confidential, I should put an ad in the *Toronto Star*'s personal column reading, "Mary come home, all is forgiven." I entered the ad as instructed. I then received a second letter giving details about the story of a certain Douglas Woods who was then in jail as a result of being framed by two police officers.

The two officers had posed as criminals and had threatened to beat up Woods if he did not break into the marina where he worked and steal a number of outboard motors. Woods complied and, as he emerged, the two officers arrested him and charged him with theft.

Woods had been convicted in court and sentenced to one year in jail and he had been refused legal aid to enter an appeal. By the time I heard of all this, he had spent eight months behind bars. I was shocked at the story, and when I related it in the Legislature, the Attorney General quickly intervened, sending the matter to the Court of Appeal and within a few days Woods was free.

One month later I received a third letter saying that if I would be at the phone in the west lobby of the Parliament Buildings at 9:00 AM the following day, my informant would contact me. I received the call as promised and a male voice instructed me that if in future I wanted confidential information from the Justice Department, I should leave my daily legislative record open on my desk any Thursday evening when I left the Parliament Buildings and be at this particular phone the following morning at 9:00. He would then call me and attempt to supply the required information.

Over the next eighteen months my mysterious informant did supply me with information in several cases and it invariably turned out to be accurate. He appeared to have access both to the office of the Justice Department and to the intelligence files of the Provincial Police.

My new contact proved to be invaluable when, on February 6, 1970, Mrs. Elizabeth Citron, an attractive young brunette from Burlington, Ontario, came to my office in the Legislature to tell me what appeared to be on the surface an unbelievable tale. She complained that she had been threatened with a gun by her next door neighbour, one George Clinton Duke, a wealthy industrialist who had warned her not to go to the authorities because of his close connections with the police. Mrs. Citron told me that Duke not only had many friends in the police and wore an official police tie pin, but was also personally friendly with three men who had lengthy criminal records involving heroin smuggling and other activities of organized crime. I found her story hard to believe but decided to check it out on the off chance that there might be some truth to it. And so I took advantage of my pipeline to the office of Attorney General Arthur Wishart.

Following Mrs.Citron's visit, I contacted my informant and asked him if he could find out anything about Mr. Duke and his relationship with the police and/or the Mafia. The story he brought me back the following week was even more shocking than Mrs. Citron's. It seemed that Duke had a very serious criminal record as a youth but had been going straight for some twenty-eight years. Recently he had become very close with a number of senior police officers. He had even dined with the Commissioner of the force who had given him the present of a police tie pin. As a result of his friendship with senior OPP officers, Duke was able to have driving offences withdrawn or reduced. Moreover, there had been a report from the Chief of Police of the nearby city of Hamilton that Duke was associating with known Mafia characters and that because of his relationship with the police it

was becoming difficult to carry on normal law enforcement in the area.

I immediately took Mrs. Citron's charges to the Legislature. If it had not been for the ineptitude of Attorney General Arthur Wishart, the whole matter would have been finished that day, for, after all, it was pretty minor stuff as scandals go. A few police officers would have been disciplined and my career as a Mafia irritant would never have started. But I think that Wishart's dislike of me coloured his response. He asked for two weeks to investigate the matter and then produced a report saying that my charges were baseless. Unfortunately for Wishart the report had been drawn up hastily and was full of omissions and errors. It gradually fell apart as the Justice Committee examined it paragraph by paragraph.

• The Attorney General stressed in his report "that there had been no significant contact between Mr. Duke" and mobster Johnny Papalia. Wishart was shocked into silence when I revealed that the Chief of Police in Hamilton had received a complaint from Duke's wife that she feared for her life from Papalia because of things that had taken place in the Duke home.
• The Attorney General stated flatly that Duke had never used influence to have traffic charges withdrawn. I found this hard to believe and asked Mr. Wishart, "Tell me, in the course of your investigation with Mr. Duke's driving problems, have you found that there were any cases where police officers were going to lay charges but the charges were not laid?" The Attorney General replied, "No. There was no suggestion and no evidence of charges not being laid." I then asked, "Were there ever cases where an officer wished to lay charges and his superior officer told him not to do so?" At this, OPP Commissioner Eric Silk jumped in to reply, "Certainly not."

Later it turned out that: (1) A recommendation for a

careless driving charge against Duke made by an OPP constable and his corporal simply "disappeared" from the OPP offices and later the OPP records were falsified to make it appear that a magistrate had withdrawn the charge. (2) A summons for speeding at 80 m.p.h. was reduced to a lesser charge in order to save Duke from a loss of four demerit points because "he was transporting a gun to the widow of an OPP inspector." (3) A speeding ticket for driving 75 m.p.h. vanished after the probationary policeman who had stopped Duke was called in for a little chat with his sergeant.

• Mr. Wishart glossed over Duke's OPP pin, saying it could be purchased anywhere for fifty cents. He was mightily embarrassed when it turned out that the Commissioner of the force had personally given it to Duke.

• Finally, the Attorney General flatly stated that no OPP officer had ever received gifts from Duke. This too turned out to be untrue.

All this produced great delight on the opposition benches and front-page headlines day after day in the press. Finally, to stop the uproar, Premier John Robarts ordered a Royal Commission to investigate the matter. Well, sort of. He ordered the commission to investigate "any improper relationships between OPP personnel and three particular ex-criminals (other than Duke). Cute – because I hadn't made any such allegations.

The commission hearings were a nightmare for me as the lawyers went to work to discredit me. I soon found myself defending all sorts of incidents in my past life that had nothing to do with the hearing. Lawyers for the OPP, Duke and the criminals cross-examined me on everything from the Parker Royal Commission on coroners to speeches I had made on the government's housing policies, to a law suit on stock options in which I had been a witness. They all took their best shot at me.

Harvey Daiter, the lawyer for Duke, said, "Didn't you

go off half cocked? You have a record of making baseless allegations."

John Bowlby read Judge Parker's report in which he called me a McCarthyite.[1] When I replied, "That sounds like Parker," Commissioner Judge Campbell told me, "I don't want you making any more remarks about members of the bench."

It seemed to be open season on Morton Shulman. Every detail of my own life was up for examination but, when Johnny Papalia's bodyguard, Red Lebarre, took the stand and I tried to ask him about a meeting Lebarre had had with Mafia boss Meyer Lansky, this was ruled "not pertinent" to the inquiry and Mr. Lebarre was told not to answer.

The OPP lawyer was most anxious to determine my sources of information and, when I refused to reveal them, he demanded that I be jailed. The commissioner denied him this pleasure but Inquiry Counsel J.J. Robinette said, "I intend to bring the facts to the attention of the Crown Attorney for Metropolitan Toronto . . . on Dr. Shulman's own evidence there is grave probability that he has been guilty of a criminal offence . . . A police force with confidential information in its secret files cannot operate efficiently if the contents of these files are going to be systematically leaked to a member of the House or anyone else." He said I might get five years in jail.

The commissioner did his best with the restrictive terms of reference. After a complete investigation, he ultimately ruled that there had been no improper relationship between the OPP and known criminals. He suggested that "Dr. Shulman's admitted acts of securing secret and confidential information from his informant may render him guilty to prosecution as well."

The commissioner made an interesting slip. He meant, of course, *liable* to prosecution. Attorney General

[1] See *Coroner*, page 150.

Wishart announced that he wished to "pursue" that suggestion.

Harvey Daiter announced that he hoped to launch Legislature disciplinary proceedings against me. He said he would draw up a list of charges "based on Shulman's career" and refer them to the Legislature Speaker for submission to the committee on privileges. "If the committee sees fit, they can take away his privilege of immunity, suspend him or have him impeached."

The *Toronto Star* summed it up this way:

An inquiry that is asked to discover the truth or untruth of allegations that were never made is not likely to come to a very useful conclusion. And the laconic conclusion of Mr. Justice Campbell Grant, replying negatively to the two questions put to him by the Robarts' government, is probably the least useful part of his report on the "Commission of Inquiry re Ontario Provincial Police."

The main body of the report is much more enlightening than the conclusion, and it is not a whitewash of the OPP at either the top or lower levels. Mr. Justice Grant says it was "indiscreet" of senior officers to have accepted Christmas presents from Duke's company, which was selling the force lawn equipment. He also finds a failure in discretion by OPP Commissioner Eric Silk, who "clothed Duke with approval" on brief acquaintance by inviting him to lunch with senior OPP personnel. The report also notes embarrassing faults in the OPP's filing system and internal communications. A subordinate failed to tell Mr. Silk of Duke's criminal record; some records on Duke mysteriously disappeared. A senior officer "would have been more discreet" to consult the Crown Attorney and act on his advice rather than deciding on his own not to proceed with a careless driving charge against Mr. Duke. We think Mr. Justice Grant might well have taken a sterner view of such indiscretions, which could shake the public's confidence in the integrity of the police.

Attorney General Arthur Wishart says he will study the report to see if Dr. Shulman should be prosecuted. We advise him to forget that, and start explaining why the government fouled up its instructions to the commissioner.

It was all very sad and disillusioning for me. The only results were that two officers were temporarily suspended from the police force while I had three libel and slander suits brought against me. Perhaps I should have quit then. But I had the bug – and as a result of the publicity, police informants began to come to my office. Soon I was receiving regular information on police investigations which mysteriously had not led to charges.

In May 1970 I gave a series of speeches outlining organized crime's involvement in the construction industry and their links with both the Liberal and Conservative parties.

Among the matters I disclosed were:

• That the OPP was totally incompetent to handle organized crime. A secret report prepared for the government by the efficiency expert firm of Hickling Johnston read, "The efficiency level of the OPP up to staff sergeant is very good, but the efficiency in the higher levels is deplorably bad, in inverse proportion to the level of the position."

To cite just one example of this inefficiency: The FBI had informed the OPP that a key meeting was to take place at Toronto's Inn on the Park between a number of top U.S. crime figures. The OPP carefully staked out the hotel. But they learned nothing because they did not know what their quarry looked like as pictures had not been distributed to the officers. In this situation, the police did their best taking down the licence numbers of all the cars. But the next day they discovered they were all owned by Avis! (In the midst of all this bumbling, the playboy son of a Toronto newspaper publisher more or less innocently attempted to pick up the beautiful young mistress of the elderly Carlo Gambino and had his arm broken for his pains. The police advised him not to lay charges.)

• The Ontario Police Commission had submitted a report in February 1970 to the Attorney General saying that organized crime was out of control in Ontario and requesting that a Royal Commission bet set up to look into the problem. This report had been kept secret. When I revealed its existence, Attorney General Wishart was apoplectic.

• Phony unions had been set up in the construction industry by a number of contractors in league with several crooked labour leaders. A few honest labour leaders were threatened or beaten and contractors who did not sign up with the unions had their equipment damaged and fires set on their jobs. Individual workers who objected to the low pay or lack of a real union were warned that they had better stay in line or they would be visited by one Johnny Papalia. Illegal phony strikes were organized by the contractors themselves, who used these strikes as a pretext to extract more money from the builders.

• Key meetings had taken place in Toronto between Mafiosa strongmen and crooked union leaders on the one hand, and representatives of the major Toronto builders on the other. One of the builders present was a former Liberal candidate. At the meetings the builders agreed to order their employees to join the new phony unions in order to forestall a real union coming in later on. They also hired a private detective to make sure that there was no opposition from the international unions. And they gave this detective instructions to beat up certain representatives of these unions.

• A dozen men were instructed to appear before Ontario's Labour Relations Board and to perjure themselves as to how the unions had been set up.

• Toronto's Chief of Police had prepared a report listing many of the violent acts in Toronto and sent it to

the Ontario Police Commission who in turn had sent it
on to the Attorney General with another request for a
Royal Commission. But the Attorney General had rejected this request and decided to sit tight.

• I named all the persons involved with no fear of libel
suits because of my parliamentary immunity and the
press printed it all. The Attorney General, the government, the Liberals and the crooks were all furious.

On June 6, 1970 I gave the last of these speeches and
then departed on a long-planned holiday in Italy. As I
was leaving, Donald MacDonald, then still NDP leader,
asked where I was going and I replied in jest, "To investigate the Mafia in Sicily." I could not have made a worse
joke for MacDonald took me seriously and at a press
conference the next day repeated my statement to the
press. Three days later I phoned home from Palermo to
be told that the papers were full of speculation about
my "Sicilian adventure." I was appalled but decided I
had better get some pertinent information to bring back.
I approached my hotel manager and asked if it would be
possible to meet the local Mafia chief. I am sure that he
thought I was out of my head but he decided to take
advantage of the crazy tourist and so in return for payment of 50,000 lire ($43 U.S.) I was driven out of the
city, up a country road to the top of a little mountain
where I was duly introduced to a short, shabby, furtive
man who claimed to be the number one boss of the local
Mafia. Alas, he spoke no English and my interpreter
translated that he knew nothing of criminal activities in
Canada.

While I was participating in this low comedy in Sicily,
more serious activities were taking place in Toronto.

On June 17, 1970 an undercover RCMP officer phoned
his superior at headquarters to inform him, "There's a
contract out on Shulman. They have had enough of his
trouble making." The RCMP inspector immediately noti-

fied Metro police and this resulted in two senior officers arriving at my home to offer protection.

It was hot in Palermo on June 18, 1970, so I had taken an afternoon rest and gone out for a late dinner. When I returned to the decrepit hotel at eleven o'clock, the desk clerk said, "Someone has been calling you from Canada all evening. They are on the line now." I picked up the phone in the lobby and through the bad connection heard my wife's strained voice: "There are two police officers here and they say that the Mafia has put out a contract on your life – please catch the first plane and come home at once."

It was a terrible shock to receive the news that "they" were after me while I was in their very heartland. I

couldn't understand it: all I had done was give a few speeches in the Legislature about organized crime and what I had said did not seem to me to be that important. Whether I deserved this attention or not, flight was obviously advisable. I ran up to my hotel room, packed, paid my bill and took a taxi to the airport. The next plane north would not leave for eight hours and I spent the time huddled in a corner of the waiting room, nervously eyeing every man who came through the door.

When I finally reached Toronto, I was greeted by the two Metro detectives who informed me that a twenty-four hour a day guard had been assigned to me and my home. For the next two weeks I was accompanied everywhere I went by bodyguards. At first I found it rather fun, but after a few days the fun paled, for all privacy disappeared. Every person I visited or party I attended had extra uninvited police guests. And every time I went to a restaurant, the officers would demand that I reserve under a phony name and even then they would insist on searching the kitchen.

After fourteen days had passed, the original detectives visited me and, to my great relief, informed me that they had succeeded in having the Mafia contract cancelled. I would, therefore, no longer need a police guard. I pressed the officers for details but they insisted that they were not allowed to give them to me. Later, one of my RCMP informants told me that the contract had been placed by a Toronto businessman whom I had named as a Mafia member in the Legislature. But the word of my anticipated demise had got out prematurely and as a result of the intense "heat" this had produced, the businessman had been visited by a local "enforcer" who had "persuaded" him that my death would produce more harm than good.

Despite the withdrawal of their guard, the police were not entirely sanguine. They issued me a rare permit to carry a concealed pistol, and I outfitted myself with a small .25 calibre automatic. I carried it for some months, despite my wife's complaints that my suits were all sagging out of shape, until one day a friend chided me, "Morty, do you really think someone is going to come up to you and say 'Draw!'?"

After my return from Italy, I was approached by one Clayton Ruby, a local lawyer. Ruby had been dating my secretary and through her he sent word that he had heard that I was interested in information about organized crime and that I would soon be contacted by a private detective named Max Chikofsky who had information which would be of value to me. The next day Chikofsky phoned me and said that he had much information and documentation. He wanted to supply this to me "as a public spirited citizen" – he wanted no money. He refused to come to either my office or home and we finally agreed to meet that night at the midtown home of my secretary.

Chikofsky was very much cloak-and-dagger. I arrived at the appointed hour and ten minutes later the detective knocked at the door. He then told me that he had come an hour earlier and had been watching the house to make sure I was not followed. My amusement at Chikofsky's caution soon evaporated as he poured out a story of crime and violence in the construction industry. Any doubts I had were dissipated when he produced a mass of documents to back up his allegations. Not only did Chikofsky have details and material from labour sources, he also had information which could only have come from the police.

I gratefully accepted all this material and soon began a new series of speeches in the Ontario Legislature which were, to great extent, based on Chikofsky's documents. The information he gave me proved 100 per cent accurate. For two years we met at irregular intervals and on each occasion he supplied me with more confidential material. I could not get over my good fortune at making this contact. Little did I know what a disaster it was later to lead to.

15 *Libel*

In my eight years in the Legislature I was sued countless times: by alleged Mafiosa, furious physicians, angered private detectives and even by a Toronto reporter who accused me of alienating his wife's affections – apparently through the media since I never actually met the lady. He sued for $100,000,000. But the most bizarre case of all involved the Attorney General and a judge of the Ontario provincial court.

In the middle of the Mafia threats and allegations, documentary evidence including photographs were brought to me showing that a senior Ontario judge had taken a holiday in a resort owned by a wealthy Toronto man with reputed gangster associations, and that the judge's bill had been paid by the businessman. This in itself was not evidence of corruption. But, in my view, it merited further investigation which I did not personally have the facilities to carry out. I could have raised the matter in the Legislature where my words would have been protected by immunity but this, I felt, would be unfair to the judge. Instead, I sent a personal and confidential letter to the Attorney General requesting that he investigate the matter.

Amazingly, Arthur Wishart promptly photostated my letter and gave a copy to the judge who in turn gave a copy to the businessman. The next day I was sued for one million dollars by that businessman.

A phenomenal storm broke over Wishart's indiscretion. As Harold Greer observed in the *Montreal Star*, "It raises questions not only about Mr. Wishart's competence as Attorney General but even more fundamentally about the rights, duties and privileges of a parliamentarian (or any other citizen for that matter) in giving confidential information to the government without laying himself open to an action for libel." But despite all the screaming, the law suit succeeded in what I assume was its purpose: the matter became *sub judice* so that I was unable to discuss the details in the Legislature. And, since the case was not pursued, the facts were never made public.

In fact, oddly enough, *none* of the libel suits was ever pursued. At first I would phone my lawyer enthusiastically asking, "When are we going to court?" but it gradually sank in that no one ever intended to go to court – only to shut me up. Many of these cases, in fact, are still pending to this day.

'HERE COME THE JUDGE!'

16 *Arsenic and Old Tories*

While these other matters were progressing, I became involved in a public health problem which still plagues Ontario. In April 1970, I received a letter from a resident of Deloro, a tiny town in eastern Ontario, complaining that arsenic was being discharged into the Moira River and Lake from an old abandoned refinery. The poison level was so high that cows drinking from the lake had died. The writer went on to say that complaints to Ontario's Water Resources Commission had received no response whatsoever.

I drove down to Deloro and found an amazing sight: 400,000 tons of bright blue tailings covering some fifty acres were lying in a huge dump beside the Moira River. Streams of blue tinted water ran steadily from the dump into the river. And through it all stood long dead trees and vegetation, all petrified by the copper and arsenic. The residents of Deloro were in no personal danger for they all drank well water, but everyone downstream was at risk.

The Ontario Water Resources Commission had said that the safe level of arsenic was 0.05 parts per million but tests of the surface water ran at 0.42 parts per million. And the water at the bottom of Moira Lake read at an incredible and lethal 400 parts per million. Several medical studies, dating back to 1929, had shown that drinking water with arsenic in it or even swimming in such water can produce cancer. Therefore, I went down to the vital statistics department and examined the cancer rate for that area (Hastings, Frontenac and Prince Edward counties). I discovered that it was rising 75 per cent faster than the rest of the province.

Moira Lake then had three hundred cottages on its shores, eight tourist establishments and two boys' camps. It seemed to me that I had stumbled onto something of terrible and urgent importance. I went to the Legislature and demanded immediate action, but I was astounded by the response.

Dr. C. R. Link, the local Medical Officer of Health issued a statement, "In my opinion and in the opinion of the Ontario Water Resources Commission and the Department of Public Health there is no danger of people developing cancer." Energy and Resources Minister George Kerr said, "The lake water is drunk only by a small proportion of the cottagers . . . and there is no danger involved in swimming." Health Minister Tom Wells said, "The incidence of cancer in Hastings and Frontenac Counties is slightly below the average for the province of Ontario." He went on that "the levels of arsenic in Moira Lake are no longer considered a health hazard." The two ministers also issued a common statement: "There is no evidence to substantiate charges by Dr. Morton Shulman that residents of the Moira River watershed are in danger. . . ."

Things simmered down for a few days and then a report was leaked by an unhappy official in the Water Resources Commission which flatly contradicted the reassurances from the two ministers. This report stated that the concentration of the arsenic was ten times the safe level for human consumption. Suddenly George Kerr got the message. In a statement on June 5, 1970, he said that the government was taking action against the refinery "which will require it to eliminate all leaching certainly this year." He concluded, "We are getting the necessary evidence with the idea of placing the company under a ministerial order. It is also quite possible that we will prosecute the company."

I was quite satisfied with Kerr's statement, but unfortunately I had been totally taken in. No prosecution ever took place. More important, neither did the arsenic leaching cease. Seven years later, after I had left the Legislature, I discovered that the arsenic was *still* heavily running into the Moira system and in 1977 Minister Kerr promised a cleanup for 1978. As of this writing, nothing has been done.

It turned out that Wells' comments about the cancer rates were just about as accurate as George Kerr's original statement. In January 1978, Michael Rychlo, a water quality engineer with the Ontario Ministry of the Environment, published a book called *The Arsenic Papers*. I was not too surprised to read the following:

> Claims by one doctor of increased cancer mortality rates in Hastings county due to the arsenic levels in the waters there were dismissed on the basis that the doctor was misinformed as to the statistics. Health officials referred to the publications of Ontario Vital Statistics to show that the claims were unsubstantiated. The health experts listed 77 deaths from all malignancies in 1971 for Hastings, which was supposed to make the rate for that county 83 deaths per 100,000. However, what the experts failed to include was the number of female deaths which was 68. The 77 deaths stated were only for males.
>
> The correct total meant that Hastings did in fact show a death rate higher than the provincial average. If the rates were inspected again for 1972, it would have been demonstrated that Hastings had a death rate from cancer much higher than the Ontario average.

In matters of public health as in politics it is not

enough just to be right. You must, in addition, get your message to the public. In the case of the arsenic and cancer danger in Eastern Ontario, I failed to reach and alarm enough people.

I was far more successful, however, in a battle with the highways department. Back in my days as Chief Coroner I had become familiar with highway flaws and dangers through an investigation of deaths on Toronto streets. I had fought with the city's bureaucrats to produce improvements in construction of Toronto's freeways. Now as an MPP I noticed with amazement that Ontario's new Macdonald-Cartier Freeway (Highway 401) was being constructed with the very same errors that had plagued Toronto's Don Valley expressway: hazardous and unprotected highway signs, misplaced guard rails with deadly open ends and badly placed light poles.

I photographed these flaws and took blow-ups to the Legislature where I confronted and challenged the unhappy Minister of Highways, George Gomme. Gomme didn't reply directly but to my great delight his deputy issued a statement the next day saying, "It is obvious that Dr. Shulman has been doing his homework. These defects will be corrected." And they were.

These serious efforts to improve society were dotted with episodes of low comedy. In early 1970, reports of heavy metal contamination of Ontario's sport fish began to hit the headlines, partly from my own Moira River research but primarily through the speeches of Stephen Lewis about mercury in the rivers of Northern Ontario. In order to reassure the public, the Liberal and Tory members of the Legislature from the resort areas held a fish fry at Queen's Park serving fish from their constituencies. They invited several hundred MPPs and civil servants. They happily pointed out that "All the MPPs are eating the fish and no one is dropping dead." I didn't attend the feast but I did send my secretary with orders to steal a fish which we promptly sent over to the S.E. Young Research Laboratories for analysis. The result showed a mercury content of 1.8 points per million, some eight times the safe level.

The response of the Liberal organizer for the fry, Donald Patterson, was to accuse me of putting mercury in the fish. And Conservative cabinet minister René Brunelle said, "Someone at the fish fry that night had taken some of the fish and put it in their pocket. Since people don't normally do that we took the precaution of taking some samples from the dinner ourselves for testing." But the results of these "tests" were never made public, at least to my knowledge. No further fish fries were held at Queen's Park.

Another amusing incident involved public works minister J.R. Simonett. It was an open secret at Queen's Park that everyone who did business with the government was expected to make a donation to the Conservative party. But proving this was next to impossible. I carried out an experiment, listing two printers with Public Works who wanted a share of the government's business. One of them I gave $500 to donate to the Tories while the other did not make a donation. The former received $25,000 worth of business the first year and continues to do heavy business with the government to this day, while the other was given nothing. My problem was that at the end of the year my first printer begged me not to name him. He said he needed the work and gave me back my $500.

I made the best of a bad situation and named the second printer. The ministry explained that he had been overlooked and promptly gave him a $300 order. But he would never get another one. I gave up that battle, but only after making a total ass of myself. A government employee had brought me a list of the printing firms who were on the favoured list to receive government business and I saw to my amazement that one of them was owned by the Communist party. I made the mistake of pointing out this anomaly publicly and both the *Toronto Star* and the *Globe* responded with editorials comparing me to Senator Joe McCarthy.

I did far better in a sudden raid on Ontario's St. Thomas Psychiatric Hospital. I had received a tip that some patients were going hungry at that institution because of a new incentive system. I drove there unannounced on Tuesday morning accompanied by my bright and aggressive girl Friday, Barbara Hill.

We found that the director of the hospital was attempting to motivate patients by paying them "tokens" for good behaviour and for in-hospital work. These tokens were then used to pay for their food. Those who didn't earn enough tokens were denied their meals. The regulations stated that patients had to pay one token for breakfast and two tokens each for lunch and supper. To qualify for occupational therapy or to buy candies or cigarettes, patients had to earn twenty-five tokens a week. And to take part in off-ward recreation such as movies or bingo, patients had to earn thirty tokens per week.

Patients were paid two tokens for making a bed properly, one token for brushing teeth after every meal, one for dressing properly and another for neat grooming while those earning twenty-five or more tokens a week in this way were allowed ward jobs such as sweeping the floor which paid nine tokens a day.

The problem was that these were mentally ill people and many of them were totally incapable of carrying out even the simple functions required to earn tokens. For example, one man's hands shook so badly that he could never do his bed neatly enough to earn the tokens and as a result was missing two out of three meals in a day. He had reached the point where, as a result of lack of food, he was too weak to work and without working he could not earn enough tokens for his meals.

I was outraged and rushed back to the Legislature to denounce Health Minister Tom Wells who responded:

"This treatment is used with longer term patients who sometimes have lost all initiative. The department has instructed that there is to be a thorough backup program to ensure that no patient suffers physical harm through loss of a meal . . . Shulman's report is typical Shulman – sweeping statements that have no basis in reality at all."

The next day the incentive program was cancelled.

17 *Shulman's Raiders*

In June 1970 I was approached by six high school students who had read about the U.S. consumer advocate, Ralph Nader's "raiders" and who volunteered to do the same type of work for me. I jumped at their offer, since my entire staff then consisted of two secretaries and a part-time detective and we were swamped.

The previous year I had received reports from the U.S. indicating that asbestos workers might develop cancer years later as a result of their work. When my colleague, Fred Burr, had asked questions in the House, the government had glossed this over. Then in May 1970 an article appeared in the American Medical Association Journal stating that asbestos used in construction was a greater cancer threat, both to workers and the public, than cigarettes. It seemed a great place to start my young volunteers and I put them to work on it. Six weeks later they produced a report stating that:

(1) There was no specific legislation in Ontario to control the use of asbestos.

(2) The regulations concerning noxious gases were not being uniformly enforced.

(3) Employers were not required to get any permit for the use of asbestos or even to notify the labour department.

(4) On many construction sites the asbestos was being sprayed into the air and was contaminating areas for blocks about.

(5) The public (and my researchers) were denied access to specifications for building construction at Toronto City Hall.

Ontario's Health Department pooh-poohed the whole thing and Dr. V. L. Tidy, Chief of the Occupational Health Branch said that "asbestos in the air near construction sites would seem not to be a significant health hazard to passersby."

Looking back now, eight years later, it is hard to believe how aggressively the Tory government fought against restrictions on asbestos. Today it is agreed by all that minimal asbestos exposure can cause cancer and the Workmen's Compensation Board accepts claims from cancer victims who were asbestos workers. But asbestos is still commonly used in industry and in construction, masks are still not routinely used, the public air is still routinely contaminated near construction sites and the government has long forgotten my suggestions that they enact their own version of the New York law requiring the use of canvas shields during asbestos spraying.

As for my young volunteers, I reluctantly disbanded them in the fall. The government had proved so hostile to their existence that they were refused even the simplest request. As their second project I had assigned them to investigate Ontario's illegal bail bondsmen. As a start, I suggested that they go through the court records to see if there was a pattern of a few people putting up bail for hundreds of criminals. But the minute Attorney General Wishart learned of the project he ordered that the records be locked up and access be denied. When I protested, he replied, "If the particular files in question were opened the affairs of particular individuals will be disclosed in a manner that is quite inconsistent with the preservation of their rights."

Wishart and I have both since left politics – but professional bail bondsmen continue to flourish in Ontario.

18 *Liquor*

One of my very few heroes was Jim Mackey, Toronto's Chief of Police in the postwar years. Mackey did an admirable job in that post. There is no doubt in my mind that he was largely responsible for Toronto remaining an island of law and order while every other big city in North America became saturated with muggings, bank robberies and other violent crimes. Unfortunately in the mid-sixties, Mackey retired as police chief and was appointed head of the Liquor Licence Board of Ontario. In this post he was not such a success. Barely a month went by that I did not receive a complaint about some strange high-handed action by one of his inspectors. I became incensed and related some of these stories to the Legislature.

• Ed Mirvish opened a restaurant called Ed's Folly where one could dance to the music of the thirties, have a drink and order 25-cent hot dogs. The LLBO okayed the music and the liquor but ordered the hot dogs removed as "too low class."
• At Julie's singles bar in downtown Toronto, patrons moved freely about the premises talking to each other. The LLBO ordered that this must cease and no one could drink standing up.

• One LLBO inspector walked into a restaurant called the Coal Bin and decided there were too many tables. He would not wait until closing time but ordered the manager to drag out the tables and chairs even though patrons were seated at them.

• The LLBO had ordered that no one could drink liquor in a restaurant without ordering a meal. At Julie's, if someone ate downstairs and then went up to the lounge for a drink, the inspectors ruled that this was the same as entering a new establishment and the patron had to order another meal!

• An LLBO inspector entered a restaurant called Nepantha on a Sunday and found people actually dancing and enjoying themselves. He ordered this stopped at once. When the owner objected that no liquor was served on Sundays, the inspector replied that that didn't matter: no one could dance in a *licensed* establishment on a Sunday whether or not liquor was present!

• In Hamilton, one tavern owner was ordered to replace his waitresses with men because it was "immoral" for women to serve men in a beverage room (and to heck with Ontario's law against sexual discrimination).

• At Toronto's Park Plaza Hotel, an LLBO inspector discovered free peanuts at the tables and ordered this practice of enticing the customers stopped immediately.

• A shocked LLBO inspector entered a Greek nightspot called the Neraida and to his horror found one of the entertainers dancing on a table. The LLBO promptly issued an order to the Neraida forbidding live entertainment and ordering them in future to have only recorded background music.

• In the Heritage Inn in Toronto's east end the proprietor had installed a dart board in the Game Room. The Board ordered the dart throwing stopped immediately as this was not permitted in licensed premises.

• At the Stratford Festival, liquor was allowed to be sold to persons watching the live shows but not to those watching films. Apparently the Board believed movie watchers were corrupted more easily.

• Inspectors for the Board discovered two people playing backgammon at Pips restaurant and threatened the owner with loss of his licence if it happened again.

• The LLBO issued orders to all establishments with liquor licences that they could no longer use the word "drink" in their advertisements. However, the word "drinks" was okay.

• One Spanish restaurant, El Cid, was ordered not to sell Sangria, a weak Spanish mixture of fruit and wine, while other restaurants like Café Madrid and Don Quixote continued to sell this product. When I asked John Clement, the minister responsible for the LLBO, about this particular idiocy, he replied, "Who wants to drink that cheap Spanish wine?" Chief Mackey replied a little more formally, "Under regulation 563, item 9, section 4, any non-alcoholic liquor that is added to liquor in the preparation of a drink shall be added in full view of the customer and Sangria is prepared before it reaches the customer." I pointed out to the Legislature that if that rule were to be followed strictly it would be the end of every mixed drink starting with Bloody Marys.

• At a restaurant named the New Windsor there was a "happy hour" where the patrons could get two beers for the price of one and a half. An inspector ordered the restaurant to cease this practice forthwith or be closed for six days. When the owner remonstrated that many establishments did this the inspector replied, "We are not discussing the rest of the city. We are discussing you. If the happy hour continues after today you will be suspended." The owner reluctantly complied but became increasingly frustrated as a competing watering hole, the Friars, ran a nightly ad for its "happy hour." I phoned the Liquor Board to complain and they responded by ordering the unfortunate Friars not to use the word "happy" in their ads either.

• The Board discovered that people of the opposite sex were *talking* to each other while sitting around pianos in Toronto piano bars, A.J.'s, La Strada and the Oyster Bar. The Board ordered the pianos removed immediately.

• One Toronto restaurant, Tanaka's, had very little lunch business and so decided to close until supper. They were immediately threatened with loss of their licence under Section 34c of regulation 563 of the Board which stated that in every dining lounge lunch must be served. Meanwhile, a few blocks away another dining lounge named Barberians never opened for lunch.

• A new restaurant called Marika's Café opened with partitions between the booths. The Board ordered the partitions removed because of a regulation which stated that every patron in a licensed establishment must be able to see all the other patrons in the room. At the same time, Ed Mirvish's huge restaurant, Ed's Warehouse, put in private curtained "courting parlours" where no one could see what the couple inside were doing. The LLBO inspectors did not object.

• At Oktoberfest, the annual beer celebration in Kitchener, the LLBO ordered the removal of all signs carrying pictures of a beer bottle.

• In Grey South, the LLBO rejected all applications for liquor licences for the local apple blossom festival.

• A Brazilian Carnival Charity Ball which raised money for Cardinal Leger's work in Africa, was held at Toronto's Royal York Hotel. The LLBO banned TV cameras on the ground that people should not be filmed drinking alcoholic beverages.

• Most new restaurants had to wait six months to get a liquor licence. A few mysteriously received it on the day they opened.

I made these revelations in a series of speeches to the Legislature spread out over many months and the government reacted at first with amusement, then embarrassment and finally with annoyance at the continued irritation. The newspapers played up the stories and it became too much for the Premier who called in Chief Mackey and asked for his resignation.

I wasn't very happy with my victory. The Liquor Licence Board obviously needed shaking up, but Jim Mackey was truly a good man, attempting to maintain the high moral standards of his youth. It was just a damn shame for him that he happened to be in that particular job in a time of changing mores.

While the licensing of enterprises that sell liquor by the glass comes under the Liquor Licence Board of Ontario, the importation and sale of liquor, beer and wine by the bottle in Ontario comes under the Liquor Control Board of Ontario. My single most amusing experience in government came in a battle with that terrible organization.

I have only one vice. I don't gamble, I don't have young mistresses, I drive a six-cylinder car and I don't squander money on clothing or other extravagances. I rarely drink hard liquor, and have never drunk beer. But I confess to a love of good French wines, especially Bordeaux. Unfortunately this love brings me into constant contact and conflict with the LCBO.

In the wonderful province of Ontario, liquor may be imported and retailed only by the government. Up until very recent times anyone who drank wine was regarded as a drunkard of the worst kind (a common Ontario word of disapprobation is to call someone a "wino"). For many years, in order to discourage people from indulging in this vice, few wines were imported (and on those there was a 200 per cent mark up) while the government depended on the rather unpleasant taste of Ontario's native wines to keep drinking in check. If an individual wished to import wine for his own use into this province he had to have it shipped to himself in care of the LCBO who would then pass it on – after payment of Canadian customs duties, shipping charges and a modest fee to the Ontario government which was figured out by adding up the original cost plus the shipping charges plus duty and then multiplying by three. Thus, a bottle of wine starting out at four dollars in Paris would end up costing the brave importer some eighteen dollars when it finally arrived in Toronto.

At the end of 1971, I ordered twelve bottles of wine from a Bordeaux shipper. In due course I received a letter from the LCBO asking me to come down and pay their charges and pick up my wine. I phoned that morning and said I would be there by 12:00 noon but the gentleman on the phone advised me not to come at that hour. It seemed that the LCBO was working under the siesta system since they closed from 12:00 to 1:00 every day. I knew the Board had several hundred employees and I asked the clerk why they all had to be away at the same time. He explained to me that they all liked to take their lunch together. I thought this was a little odd, but it works reasonably well in Mexico so I did not want to criticize. I rushed through my office work and managed to get down to the LCBO office by 11:30 AM.

When I arrived at the Board headquarters, I found that their huge parking lot was totally filled. I thought to myself how busy they must be. Actually I was the only customer: the parking lot was kept just for employees and no spots had been allotted for customers. I went around the block a few times but could find no empty space and finally squeezed into a tiny spot right by the front door. Leaving my car, I walked into the building.

There was a uniformed commissionaire in the front lobby and the following dialogue ensued:

"I am here to pick up some wine. Where do I go?"

"Is that your car?"

"Yes."

"Well, you will have to move your car first."

"Okay. Where shall I move it to?"

"I don't care where you move it. Just move it."

"But there is nowhere to move it to. All the spots are filled."

"That's your problem.."

I thought about that one for a minute and then I said, "Well, what if I don't move it?"

"We will have the police tow it away."

"Okay, you call the police to tow it away. I just want to pick up my wine and I will be gone before the police arrive anyway. Where do I pick up the wine?"

"I'm not telling you."

On the wall a sign shows where the various offices are. I got in the elevator to push the button to go up to the third floor executive offices which I presumed was where I was to pick it up. Another fellow came running out and said, "You can't use the elevator until you've moved your car." I said, "There is no place to move the car to."

I pushed the button on the elevator and he said, "Oh no you don't," and put his foot in the door to make sure the elevator couldn't go up. I thought this was a little strange but I guessed it to be normal government procedure. I said, "Okay, if I can't use the elevator, I'm willing to abide by the rules." So I walked up the three flights.

I went up to the third floor and asked the girl on duty, "Where do I pick up my wine?"

She said, "Oh, that's down on the first floor, but you pay for it here."

So I gave her the money and said, "Where do I get it?"

"You go into the shipping department."

"Where is the shipping department?"

"Go down to the first floor and ask that fellow by the elevator where it is."

I said, "What if he won't tell me?"

She said, "Of course he'll tell you – don't be ridiculous!"

So down I went.

I said to the man by the elevator, "Where's the shipping department?" "I won't tell you" he replied.

I didn't know what to do. I thought there was no use continuing this. I went outside and there was a uniformed employee walking by.

"Do you know where the shipping department is?" I asked.

He pointed.

"Right over there."

So I got in my car and drove over.

I backed the car up to the ramp, got out and said to the attendant, "Here's my receipt; I paid for it. Can I have my wine?" Another official appeared and said, "Oh no, you can't put your car there. Move it back to where it was before. You have to enter the shipping department through the lobby." I said, "I don't know if they'll let me." He said, "Sure they'll let you. You move your car back right where it was before beside the door and come through the lobby."

So I moved the car back to where it was before, went into the lobby and said, "Where is the shipping department?"

There were two of them now, standing shoulder to shoulder. The bigger one spoke. "You're not going into the shipping department until the police arrive." At this point I thought I'd better go up and speak to whoever was in charge of this establishment. I couldn't use the elevator, so I climbed up the three floors again.

There are all sorts of offices all around the outside, and I wasn't sure which person to speak to. So I stood in the middle of the floor and, at the top of my voice, I yelled, "Who runs this madhouse?"

The executives all ran out – and several of them claimed credit for it! They took me back downstairs again and a whole bunch of them escorted me bodily into the shipping department and gave me my wine – all, that is, except three bottles which apparently had got "lost" between the time it arrived at the Liquor Control

Board and the time I had gone to pick it up. They told me at the time that they had been broken on arrival. I opened the original case but there were no wine stains or broken glass; I guess they must have evaporated.

I related this ludicrous story to the members of the Legislature and John Clement, the minister responsible, was so appalled that he ordered a shakeup at the Liquor Board. I had completed my speech by saying that my only real question was, "Why do they all have to take their lunch together?" Miraculously, within days the Liquor Board made many small changes. They opened for regular business hours, they made parking available for customers and they actually began to receive their customers politely instead of as unwanted pariahs. Since then, they have even opened a rare wine shop where an excellent selection of imported wines is available.

Sadly, they have still not changed their pricing policy. The citizen of Ontario today pays more for wine than anyone else in North America. It still infuriates me to see wines sold here at twenty dollars which are selling at eight or nine dollars a bottle just across the river in Buffalo. But one must be grateful that things are better than they were. After all, they no longer close up at lunch time.

19 *The Medical Lab Rip-off*

Doctors are unhappy with OHIP, patients can no longer get house calls, and the public purse is being bankrupted. But one group has benefited enormously from medicare and that is the lab owners. Prior to the coming of government health insurance, lab tests were ordered when needed – and, because they were expensive, *only* when needed. But since the advent of "free" (that is to say, government-paid) lab tests, their use has grown two hundred per cent.

I first learned of the racketeering involved back in September 1970 when I received a complaint from a patient who had visited a Toronto doctor with a headache. The patient had not been examined but instead referred to a lab owned by the doctor for X-rays and lab tests for which a bill of $250 was sent to OHIP. Investigation of the records showed me that the doctor was earning a modest $25,000 yearly as a physician but another $450,000 from his lab. Furthermore, this doctor was not unique. There were dozens like him scattered across the province.

On October 20, 1970 I brought the facts to the Legislature health committee. Health Minister Tom Wells said that he was aware of the situation: "As a result, it is our intention to do several things in this province in the near future. One of the things we may do is introduce licensing of laboratories and another is to change the way in which the laboratories are repaid (by the government under the OHIP scheme)."

Licensing would allow the government to say who could run laboratories. "Maybe we won't allow doctors to run them. I am not saying that that's what will happen. There may be certain areas where a doctor might have to run a laboratory, such as in remote areas of the province."

But neither Wells nor any of the succeeding Health Ministers did anything about the problem. Five years later, my successor in the High Park constituency, Ed Ziemba, repeated my charges to the Legislature with added details about kickbacks to doctors who did not own their own labs but referred patients to doctors who did. The then Health Minister, Frank Miller, promised that the law would be changed to prevent doctors referring patients to their own lab. But he too was just talking and still nothing has been done. Ed Ziemba, on the other hand, went to jail when he refused to name the source of his information about the labs in a subsequent court case.

Recently, a patient came to my office complaining bitterly that she had entered a doctor's office two blocks from mine after a fall on her rump. The doctor promptly referred her to a lab in his building for $150 worth of tests and X-rays. She was not examined. I have laid a complaint with the College of Physicians and Surgeons and the current Minister of Health, Dennis Timbrell, has promised that "soon" there will be legislation to control the problem.

It astounds me that through the incompetence of our provincial government we waste millions of dollars annually in this way.

20 *More on the Mafia*

By the end of 1970, information was pouring into my office about organized crime from my mysterious source in the Attorney General's office, from private detective Max Chikofsky and from police officers at all three levels of enforcement (city, provincial and RCMP) who were frustrated by the lack of government action against the Mafia. In October 1970 I passed on the following information to the Legislature:

- American Mafia leaders were meeting regularly at Turkey Point, Ontario with various American politicians because the heat was too great in the U.S.A.
- Organized crime had heavily infiltrated and largely taken over a segment of Ontario's construction industry.
- Large sums of money due to workers in the construction industry were being siphoned off to criminals and any protestors were threatened with violence.
- The FBI had learned, through wiretapping, of a hundred million dollar international betting ring run in Canada and the U.S. by the Magaddino family. The FBI passed all the information on to the OPP and RCMP and arranged to simultaneously raid the criminals on both sides of the border. The FBI carried out their arrests. But the parallel Ontario raids were mysteriously ordered cancelled.

- Confidential information about heroin smuggling passed by the FBI to the OPP had somehow leaked out to a Hamilton reporter who wrote the story up before the criminals could be arrested.

My revelations were greeted by fury and derision on all sides.

Attorney General Wishart stated: "Dr. Morton Shulman has done irreparable damage to police intelligence work in Ontario by claiming to have sources high in police ranks.

"He is destroying the credibility of Ontario police forces and is doing incalculable damage to the entire intelligence system which we have worked so hard to establish for the efficient exchange of information between law enforcement agencies not only in this country but throughout the world."

The city manager of Buffalo called me a charlatan and said that my naming the people at the Turkey Point meetings was "a slander and a slur on the people who live in Niagara Falls, New York."

Speaking for the Liberals, MPP Vernon Singer called me "an absolute Fascist" and accused me of using "near criminal tactics."

I learned to live with these taunts. But much worse was to come.

21 *The Future is Here*

At the end of 1970, *Toronto Calendar Magazine* approached consultant Leonard Watt, entrepreneur Roel Bramer, economist Anthony Amery, broker John Dinnick and me for a prediction of what would happen in the seventies. Looking back now, I am pleased with the overall accuracy of my predictions:

> Inflation will still be with us and it will take $2 in 1980 to buy what $1 buys today. The cost of living index will be about 50% higher in 1980 than it is today.

> The stock market is now on the way up. That magical figure of 1000 should be reached and broken by the Dow Jones Index in 1972 and generally in most areas a better economic climate will return.

> The U.S. dollar will continue to weaken and will probably be devalued late in the decade and it will be a substantial devaluation – about 50%. Gold will rise to about twice its present pegged value of $35 per ounce. Because, even with devaluation, the U.S. dollar will still be backed by gold.

> Canada's dollar will not remain free very much longer. Probably in 1971 we will see a fixed rate of exchange established again at about 96 cents.

If I were investing today for return over the next decade, I would buy convertible bonds in the oil or uranium industries. Bell Canada and the other utilities are companies whose shares won't increase much. On the other hand, such companies as IBM, General Motors and International Nickel should do very well. Anti-pollution will be the biggest growth industry of the decade.

The Liberals will be in Ottawa again in 1980, Toronto will have a population of 3.5 million and this size will cost us all about 75% more in taxes than we presently pay. The Spadina Expressway will no longer be an issue and will have reached Bloor Street where it will terminate. More tall buildings will have been built and the tallest will be around eighty storeys (*versus* fifty-seven storeys for the Commerce Court).

There will only be two newspapers in the city by 1980.

On the brighter side, the Viet Nam War will be over, there will be electric cars on the roads and girls will again be wearing the mini.

Among the other experts' predictions, Consultant Leonard Watt said:

The struggle against inflation should be resolved by the middle of the decade after which time interest rates will cease to rise. I see bank interest rates declining by 1980 to about 5½% and bond rates will decline accordingly to about 6½%.

Unemployment will lessen over the next decade with its biggest drop taking place after 1972. By 1975 it should be around 4% and by 1980 down to 3%.

Entrepreneur Roel Bramer suggested:

Most people want to be mothered from cradle to grave, so the NDP will be the obvious choice for the political party in Ottawa in 1980. With increased nationalist/ socialist interference by government, U.S. ownership will certainly play a less important role in Canadian industry by 1980.

Economist Anthony Amery said:

> Gold will remain exactly where it is all through the decade, pegged and supported at $35 per ounce. I feel that the U.S. is sufficiently committed to the present value between gold and the U.S. dollar that they will try almost anything to maintain it. Similarly, in spite of an undercurrent of speculation, the U.S. dollar will not be devalued during the next ten years and for the same reasons."

And broker John Dinnick predicted:

> Unemployment will drop to 5% by 1975 and to 4% by 1980.

> The U.S. dollar will not be devalued.

> I hope it will be the Liberals or the Conservatives in Ottawa by 1980, but fear that at some time in the future the NDP will elect a majority and this could well be by 1980.

The danger in making predictions is that some ornery person will dig them up later and remind you!

22 *Bill Davis*

My greatest aggravation in those years was in dealing with the Tory cabinet who automatically turned down any suggestion or request coming from me.

Typical was the case of Mrs. Sylvia Sapiano who injured her back at work and applied for Workmen's Compensation. She was turned down because the Workmen's Compensation Board said there was no proof that the accident had happened at work. The injured woman wasn't too disturbed because she had a policy with Occidental Life which covered everything *not* happening at work. But when she went to Occidental, they rejected her because at the WCB hearing she had stated that the accident happened at work.

I went to Bert Lawrence, Minister of Financial and Commercial Affairs, with this case. He looked into it and came back and said, in so many words, that it was very sad but obviously you couldn't blame Occidental Life because they had her own sworn testimony that it happened at work and their policy clearly stated that they covered everything *except* the things that happen at work. And you couldn't blame the Workmen's Compensation Board because they had given her a full hearing and there was no proof that it did happen at work. Her case was very sad but it fell between two stools and the insurance company had acted fairly and honourably.

Lawrence's insensitivity to others' feelings resulted in his early humiliation and retirement from politics after he made the mistake of using a government plane on a trip to Cuba. And after I made the Sapiano case public, Occidental Life suddenly changed its mind and paid the claim.

Darcy McKeough in those days was very strident and right wing and his current polish had yet to develop. One day in the Legislature I made a two hour detailed analysis of the problem of car insurance in Ontario. At the conclusion I turned to the cabinet benches and asked if I could have any comment from the cabinet. McKeough then rose to his feet and after a significant pause roared at the top of his voice, "Sleazy Morty."

The Darcy McKeough of today bears no resemblance to the man of 1970. I have never seen a politician mellow and grow as Darcy has. A personal experience illustrates how sensitive he has become to others' feelings.

Five years after the "Sleazy Morty" incident, my daughter, Dianne, graduated from law and applied for a position with the Ontario government. She, of course, used her married name on the application form, and she got the job. But the day before she was to start, the head of her department phoned her and accused her of duplicity for not revealing that she was my daughter. This, he said, changed the situation entirely. She was not to come to work until he had checked with the minister. And he said that it was the Deputy's personal opinion that she would not be acceptable.

I was enraged to think that the Tories would inflict punishment upon my daughter for the sins of her father. My first impulse was to rush down to the Legislature and denounce them. Dianne, however, cooled me down and suggested that I wait until Monday to see what Darcy McKeough, the minister concerned, would decide. On the Monday the same department head phoned Dianne and told her to come to work.

Several days later I met Darcy McKeough in the hall at Queen's Park and stopped him to thank him for hiring Dianne to which he replied, "Why Morty, if we didn't hire each others' children, who would?" I have always held a soft spot for Darcy McKeough since that time. And I made a point of never involving myself in the affairs of his department while Dianne worked there.

Allan Grossman, Minister of Reform Institutions, was another minister with whom I continued to battle. Unfortunately, I had already earned such animosity from Grossman that a number of innocent people suffered from his blanket rejection of every case I raised. For example, one of my patients got drunk in a tavern and struck a policeman. He was arrested and sentenced to fifteen days in jail which he served. This man had worked for Massey Ferguson for twenty years, and had never before been in trouble with the police. He had five children and a good reputation. But because there had been a good deal of publicity lately about policemen being attacked, the Crown appealed the fifteen-day sentence. The case went to the Court of Appeal which then raised the sentence to six months.

I wrote a letter to Grossman, explaining that Massey Ferguson would keep the man at work if he could go on the province's Temporary Absence Program and serve his sentence nights and weekends. I was sure that Grossman would agree since he had just finished a series of speeches boasting about this program. But he didn't even answer my letter and my patient was sent off to Guelph Reformatory. I phoned the department and asked why my application had been rejected and the reply was, "We don't know. They don't give reasons."

The only member of that cabinet with whom I never fought was Minister of Education Bill Davis. I knew very little about his department and didn't harass him as much as the other ministers. And in any case, Davis had the knack of turning away nasty questions with lengthy and convoluted, innocuous answers. He just wouldn't strike at the bait the way his colleagues did. In addition, Bill Davis was the ultimate politician. He was the only Tory, in or out of the cabinet, who ever visited me at Queen's Park and on several occasions he dropped into my office to chat briefly. He even laughed with me at the list of Tory cabinet ministers posted over my desk who were my current targets. As one by one they resigned or were transferred, I would put a big black X through their names.

Looking back, I guess Davis soft-soaped and conned me. I certainly took no shots at him in the House. And, when he declared for leader of the Tories on John Robarts' retirement in January 1971, I even issued a statement saying that he was the only logical choice for premier on the grounds that, if we have to have a Tory government, it should be a good one. With the benefit of hindsight I now can see what a terrible job Bill Davis did as Education Minister. He expanded the education system tenfold, keeping tens of thousands in school who might otherwise have been out apprenticing at a trade. Today too many of those young people have useless diplomas and degrees and can't get jobs. And at what cost! Leslie Frost's balanced budgets have given way to Bill Davis' monster deficits.

In any case, Bill Davis won the Tory leadership convention despite my support and began to reshape the government in his own image. He quickly neutralized Allan Lawrence, the young, aggressive Attorney General who had been his chief opponent along with Bert Lawrence (no relation) and Bob Welch, by appointing them super ministers with great titles and no power. As for the rest of the cabinet, he developed a technique of shifting his ministers from post to post at frequent intervals. This very cleverly prevented the opposition from making heavy criticism of any particular minister for after each shift the new minister would say that he had just arrived and could hardly be held responsible for his predecessors' actions! Unfortunately, this also meant that most of the ministers never did become familiar with their posts and the workings of the government were left to the civil service.

23 *Compensation for the Innocent*

As a result of all the publicity concerning my earlier cases, I had become the province's unofficial Ombudsman. Dozens of letters came to my office daily pleading for help in various problems dealing with bureaucracy. A surprising number came from convicts claiming their innocence – and some of them proved to be telling the truth. One case that impressed me greatly was that of twenty-one-year-old Fred McKenna who had been accused and jailed for bank robbery. When, six months later, he was found to be totally innocent, he was freed without so much as an "I'm sorry."

I was deeply disturbed by this and other similar cases and felt then (as I still do) that the state should compensate those whom it has wrongfully punished. I wanted to introduce a bill in the Legislature to this effect. But, since I didn't want it to die as my bills usually did, I sought advance support from the other parties. I approached Jim Bullbrook, the bright Liberal member for Sarnia, who was enthusiastic about the idea and Gordon Carton, the Conservative member from Armourdale, who, unlike many Tories, was prepared to judge issues on their merits instead of on the sponsor. Carton agreed with me that my bill made sense and he offered to co-sponsor it. Unfortunately, in February of 1971, a few weeks before my bill could be introduced, Carton was promoted to the cabinet and the Legislature's rules forbade him from co-sponsoring a private member's bill. As a substitute I met with Arthur Maloney, the well known political lawyer, my former associate in the Parkdale Conservative riding association and later to be Ombudsman for Ontario. He agreed to lend the bill his support and prestige. Encouragement also came from the press: all three Toronto papers wrote editorials supporting compensation for the convicted innocent.

The obvious problem with this concept was that everyone found not guilty by the courts is not necessarily innocent and many a guilty man has got off on a technicality. In my bill, therefore, I recommended setting up a three-man board appointed by the government to whom any aggrieved person could appeal for repayment of legal expenses and loss of wages.

Attorney General Arthur Wishart was not enthusiastic about my suggestion. But, because of the widespread press and public support (both he and I received some hundreds of approving letters), he did not reject the idea out of hand. He merely commented that most persons found "not guilty" were also "not innocent" and said that he would consider it.

Nothing was ever done.

24 *The Cages*

At the very same time I had become embroiled in yet another battle with the Health Ministry. On April 3, 1971, Lakeshore MPP Pat Lawlor and I made a surprise visit to the hospital for the retarded at Orillia as a result of a letter sent to me from a social worker. In the hospital we saw a sight I will never forget. Dozens of children were confined in cages because of lack of staff to look after them.

The hospital buildings were old and decrepit and were so crowded that in one ward the beds were so close there was no room to walk between them. In the active disturbed ward there were only three staff for twenty patients (ideally the ratio is 1:1). Some of the retarded never left their wards for exercise and most of them never received a visitor. It was like a scene from one of the old movies about horror asylums – one of the wards had eighteen beds, some with cages, in a space sixty feet by twenty-four feet. Some of the bigger children couldn't even stand up in the cages because they hit their heads on the top. One girl in a cage had her hands tied behind her.

R. J. Wilson, the administrator of the hospital admitted the charges and responded, "We'd like to get rid of those cage cots. We don't like them. If we had the staff we could probably avoid this kind of restraint. In all cases only children with strong behavioural problems are caged. There are answers to these problems but it takes time and special staff and special programs." He confirmed that some patients were confined to the cages for years, being removed only for play periods, washing and medication.

The new Health Minister, Bert Lawrence, agreed that the Orillia Hospital and the similar facility at Smiths Falls were overcrowded and behind the times and that "both have to be gradually phased out. They should be torn down as soon as funds are made available. I don't want to let the cat out of the bag but we can look forward to having these large centres replaced by smaller community-oriented treatment centres in the not too distant future."

The story was followed by widespread public outrage and outcry and words like "horror, despair and disgust" appeared in the editorials. The *Star* summed it all up by saying, "There is no excuse for any Ontarian inside or outside the government, to accept a situation in which Canada's wealthiest province fails to care decently for its sick and disadvantaged children."

The government never did close Orillia. But they immediately hired more staff and disposed of the cages.

In my political life crises came in bunches. The very same week I was battling Bert Lawrence over the crib cages, I received a phone tip from a Don Jail guard tipping me off that a man who had been charged with stealing a dime had already been held in jail for eleven days.

Reford Francottie, age forty-eight, had been arrested on April 1, 1971 and charged with taking a dime from the coin box of a newspaper stand. Francottie had no criminal record and bail was set at only $20 but he just didn't have the money and was taken to the Don. When he later appeared in court and pleaded not guilty, the Crown counsel requested and was granted a remand to

April 14 and Francottie went back to jail. The crazy thing was that, even if found guilty, Francottie would not have served more than seven days for his alleged offence.

I received the phone tip on a Saturday and went down to the Don to post bail. But I was told no bail magistrate was available that day. The next day I got Francottie out and publicized the case, demanding that Attorney General Allan Lawrence institute legislation permitting first time offenders charged with minor crimes to be released on their own recognizance.

The judge in this case, Magistrate Hugh Foster, responded to my criticisms by saying that he could not release penniless prisoners no matter how minor the charge because the accused might not return to court for trial. "If he didn't turn up it would cost the taxpayers a fortune to find him. I would be imposing a terrible outrage on the taxpayers. If there is no friend in Toronto who would trust him for $20 by posting bail, why should the court trust him?"

The Attorney General was appalled. An election was due in a few months and this was the worst kind of publicity. Never before had I got such quick results. The very next day, Al Lawrence announced that he was taking immediate steps to prevent a recurrence of such a case. Bail magistrates were put on duty seven days a week, while police were instructed to summons minor offenders rather than jail them and Crown attorneys and judges were ordered to give speedy treatment to minor cases. All in all, I was quite pleased with the outcome.

And on May 7 Reford Francottie was found not guilty!

25 *Whitby*

Sometimes I got on to scandals through the sheer stupidity of the Tories. Thus, at the beginning of May 1971 a class of nursing students at Whitby Psychiatric Hospital invited me to speak at their graduating ceremonies on May 21. A week later the embarrassed students were ordered by the Department of Health to find another speaker because "it would be quite inappropriate to have a member of the opposition speak – when the government has spent a great deal of money to develop this program."

And that should have been the end of it. But one of the students was so annoyed that she came to my office and gave me an eleven-page secret report from the hospital which said that staff morale was low and that fear dominated the nursing department.

I made haste to present the report to the Legislature and the unhappy Health Minister responded by sending an investigating team to Whitby. It turned out that most of the nursing staff were upset at the way the hospital was being run and Bert Lawrence solved the problem by transferring several senior staff members. I had no objection to this action. But I was furious a few weeks later when the government announced that they were closing the school of nursing education at Whitby Psychiatric. It smelled of revenge against the students who had talked to me. I protested but the Legislature had already closed for the summer and there was little I could do.

And once again it showed up that major government problem I have mentioned earlier. Ministers were transferred so often by Bill Davis that they never did become familiar with their departments. Oddly, the Health Ministry was the largest and most difficult branch of the government but its ministers were changed even more often than in other departments.

26 *The RCMP Papers*

It was just at this time that I became involved in one of the strangest episodes of my entire career. It had started two months earlier and hundreds of miles away.

It was 9:30 PM on the evening of May 6, 1971 in the little village of Long Sault in Eastern Ontario near the Quebec border. A tall, greying, distinguished-looking man approached the RCMP building. The five Mounties serving in the local detachment had completed their paper work and signed out at 6:00 PM. They had followed their usual custom of handing in their service revolvers to their sergeant, who locked them in the safe which also held the RCMP confidential files as well as narcotics which had been seized in a recent series of drug raids. The sergeant then double-locked the square brick building and drove off to his home. The RCMP maintained neither a night unit nor a watchman; in all the years the force had been in existence they had never suffered from a robbery in this or any other detachment.

The distinguished-looking man who boldly approached the front door of the locked station didn't look like a thief. But he was exactly that. In fact, he was a professional. Formerly an engineer, he had abandoned his profession and now worked as a break-in artist. (He later boasted to me that "I can open any lock in seconds and any safe in minutes.")

Using a gadget called a "Lockaid" he opened the Mounties' front door in less time than you or I would open our own door with a key. All he did was insert the point of the Lockaid in the door and quickly pulled the trigger five times. The pins snapped up, the lock turned and the door opened. The man stepped inside, closed the door behind him, pulled down the shades and switched on a flashlight. The old fashioned safe stood in a corner of the back office. Using a stethescope and an amplifier he had it open within five minutes. The package of heroin that he had been hired to steal was right in front and he quickly stuffed it into his briefcase. He had been told to take only that one item – but the sight of the six revolvers lying in a tray was too much for him and he quickly scooped them into his case. As an afterthought, he also took the thick pile of papers lying under the guns. These were the RCMP's confidential files.

Two weeks earlier, four RCMP officers had made a routine drug raid on a motel in the town of Cornwall, acting on a tip that a shipment of heroin had been brought in from Montreal to be sent across the border to New York. The tip was accurate. The officers confiscated $100,000 worth of heroin and arrested two heroin whole-salers, one Canadian and one American, the chief distributors of heroin in the Northeastern U.S.A. The two men had appeared for their preliminary hearings in Magistrate's Court and had been remanded on $25,000 bail for a trial to be held in September. The evidence, in the form of the bags of heroin, was only too obvious and a conviction appeared certain. On May 1, the Canadian heroin dealer had approached Tom Webster and offered him $15,000 to burgle the RCMP safe – for without the heroin there would be no evidence.

The scheme worked exactly as the crooks had hoped. The embarrassed Mounties dropped the charges and the break-in received no publicity. As an exasperated RCMP officer later put it, "Who were we supposed to report the robbery to – the local cops?"

Meanwhile, Webster delivered the heroin to the man who had hired him and collected his $15,000. He did not mention the other material he had taken for he felt this was his private find. To his amazement and delight he discovered that he had taken:

- An RCMP confidential report on organized crime in Canada, outlining which areas were vulnerable in the country and the principal Canadians involved.
- A manual revealing which buildings in Ottawa were to be guarded in case of U.S. invasion.
- A manual on how to prepare poison gases and explosives from materials readily available in the home.
- A manual on how to prevent sabotage of industry.
- Most important of all – fifty files listing all the RCMP's informants and including a master list divulging the amounts paid to each one. The list included a U.S. border guard and a number of teenagers who were being paid to spy on their fellow students.

Webster had a local reputation as a break-in artist and he expected an early visit from the police. And so, on the morning of May 7, he put all the loot in the trunk of his car and drove to Montreal where he gave it all to his friend, Stanley Norman, saying, "See what you can do with this – whatever you get we split."

On May 20, 1971 a man called my office, identified himself as André Cohen and said he wanted to sell me some information. For several months my name had been in the newspapers in connection with exposés of organized crime. As a result, this type of call was not infrequent so I did not get too excited about it. I invited the man to come to my office that afternoon. The man arrived an hour later and identified himself as Cohen. He was a mousey, nondescript, little man in his middle thirties – to me he looked like a typical clerk. He said that some of his friends had raided an RCMP station looking for machine guns but instead they had carted away "some important documents of national security. For a price they are anxious to have them returned to the federal government."

I had heard some pretty wild stories in my time and I figured that this was just one more. I smiled and suggested he send me a sample to prove that he was telling the truth. I then showed him to the door.

Four days later I arrived at my office to find a brown manilla envelope had been pushed through the mail box. Inside were two pieces of paper. One was the cover of a police manual on how to prevent industrial sabotage stamped "secret." The other was a letter from one Mountie to another saying that a local informant was to be paid $150.

I immediately called the RCMP who confirmed that a robbery had taken place at one of its detachments. The inspector said he was not entirely sure what had been taken. He asked me to get a list from Cohen of the documents he had if he phoned back.

The next day André Cohen phoned me again and set up a meeting at my medical office for six-thirty that evening. I waited until seven but he did not show up, and I left to attend a committee meeting at the Legislature. Two hours later as I was sitting in the legislative committee, a page boy brought me a note asking if I could take a phone call. When I stepped outside the room, Cohen was waiting for me. He now produced a list of the stolen documents and said he wanted $20,000 to return them plus immunity from any charges laid against him.

I contacted the police again but they said that there was no possibility of paying that kind of money. However, they urged me to string Cohen along so that they could have an opportunity to continue their investigation.

I then contacted Martin Goodman, the editor of the *Toronto Star* and asked if his newspaper would be interested in putting up some money in an attempt to buy these documents back for the police. I pointed out that in addition to doing a public service, the paper would get a great scoop. The *Star* agreed to put up $5000.

The next day I received a phone call from an official at the telephone company. He said that he was upset to learn of the obscene phone calls I had been receiving and told me that they had put a tracer on my phone to catch the man. When I expressed amazement, he said that a "nice" police officer had visited the company and told them that I had complained about receiving obscene phone calls, requesting that a tap and tracer be put on my phone.

I blew my stack and the tap was immediately taken off the telephone line. Two hours later, a police inspector phoned to apologize, explaining that there had been a "misunderstanding."

Meanwhile, Cohen called me again and said that $5000 was not nearly enough. To prove it he forwarded two RCMP documents to me which listed police informants and their pay scales.

I was tremendously shocked. I traced the first person named on the list, a seventeen-year-old youth, who told me the following story: "The RCMP came up to me as I walked home from school one day and said they knew I was involved in peddling drugs in school. I was involved in the local drug scene but I certainly was not pushing dope at school. The RCMP constable said he would pay me $85 a name for people I knew who dealed dope. He said if I did not co-operate, he would make it hard for me at school."

The youth's informing career came to a sudden end when his friends realized he was "ratting" on them. "I got punched out by six guys and left for dead in a ditch." He crawled to the road and got a ride home and told his parents that he lost his teeth in an accident. The next day a man whom he described as an "enforcer" approached him, pointed a gun at him and told him to

get out of town in twenty-four hours "or you're dead."
He changed his name and moved to Toronto.

Investigations showed that the RCMP had some dozens
of informants in the area including school boys of fifteen, sixteen and seventeen. When asked about this in
the House of Commons, Solicitor General Jean Pierre
Goyer said flatly, "The RCMP would not have a young
person as an informant on any payroll."

Six weeks later, Stanley Norman (or Cohen as he had
told me) was arrested by the OPP at the wheel of his car
in downtown Toronto. The police somehow knew to
look under the seat for the stolen papers which were
returned to the RCMP. Norman got five years, served his
time and was murdered by Montreal gangsters immediately after his release.

27 *Dirty Tricks*

As the 1971 election came nearer, my relationship with the new NDP leader, Stephen Lewis, gradually deteriorated. Neither of us had any illusions about the other. Lewis recognized that as a socialist I left much to be desired but he also knew that it was important to humour me because of my widespread voter appeal. I admired and appreciated Lewis' wit, brilliance and oratorical ability. But I had deep misgivings about his ultimate political aims. On more than one occasion we had clashed in caucus because of our conflicting views about the law, particularly where it involved labour and strikes. In one battle before he assumed the leadership, he had urged the entire NDP caucus to go to Picton and mass picket, in violation of a Supreme Court injunction. I had won that quarrel. But I had no illusions as to my ability to win any future ones now that Lewis was leader.

I approached Stephen and made one attempt at compromise. I was quite blunt and said that I didn't think we could win the election but, if we did, I wanted to ensure that the law would be carried out in the impartial way Ontario had been noted for. I therefore asked his guarantee that he would appoint me Attorney General if he won the election.

Stephen Lewis handled my demand diplomatically. He explained that he couldn't make any commitments at that point but that he would certainly give me serious consideration. The message was clear. I told him that was too bad; I would be in High Park and if he changed his mind he knew where to call me. He never did call. And so, I sat out the election in West Toronto, fighting my own private war and left Lewis and the provincial NDP to their battles elsewhere.

The election was not expected until October. But in August it was already apparent that I was going to have a fight on my hands, that it wasn't going to be the walk-over I had had the first time out. On August 9, the *Telegram* took the first shot, publishing an article on its editorial page which began:

ATTENDANCE

The second worst attender among MPPs in the Ontario Legislature is – surprise, surprise – Dr. Morton Shulman.

That's right, the same Dr. Morton Shulman who claims a record for having talked longer and on more subjects in any one session than any MPP in history. The same Dr. Shulman who complained six times in his maiden speech (March, 1968) that ministers aren't always in their seats in the House.

The same Dr. Shulman who once went into the Legislature with a camera and photographed two backbench Progressive Conservatives lolling at their desks and won huge publicity claiming they were sleeping. The same Dr. Morton Shulman who has complained time and time again that only New Democratic MPPs do a proper job of representing their constituents and that ministers fail to apply themselves to their jobs.

Dr. Shulman's failure to practise what he preaches will be revealed in detail later this week in a survey now being compiled by a political science professor at McMaster University.

Most people will be surprised to see Dr. Shulman so low on the list. No MPP gets so much publicity out of the

Legislature. What is less well known is that Dr. Shulman's strategy has been to stay around the Legislature only when there is publicity to be gained – to ask his questions and make his marathon speeches and flit before the TV cameras – and then to vanish into the distance to deal with his constituents' problems, write his books, travel on his well-paid lecture tours or just sit at home and admire his Renoirs.

On the face of it, the charge was ludicrous since I had never missed a day's attendance at the House since my election. But the *Telegram* had carefully compiled its record, not from how often I was present but by studying the percentage of *votes* I had cast. And in two years I hadn't cast a single vote because, as I noted earlier, the voting was a joke. If the Tories were about to lose a vote, the Speaker simply ruled that they had won. And, if the Opposition protested, he would simply order a "recorded" vote and stall long enough for Tory members to be pulled in from all over the city – sometimes from all over the province. On one occasion, the bells rang for four hours while absent members were flown in. I had complained bitterly about this time after time and, finally, had quit voting altogether to show my disgust.

After my initial rage at the *Telegram*'s attack, I became amused and rose in the House demanding to know how I could be only the *second* worst offender: how could anyone have a worse record if I had never voted? Everyone laughed with me. But my amusement soon disappeared as I was plunged into the political battle of my life.

The Conservative government called the election for October. The Liberals more or less wrote off High Park. For their candidate they nominated a beautiful, young, blonde law student, Laima Svegzda, 23, who had no competition for the candidacy. Miss Svegzda issued an opening statement, "I just think that it's time to get in there. I think I have a lot of things going for me. I have an ethnic background (Lithuanian). I'm young, I'm female and I have a strong feeling of what the various ethnic groups want. I haven't met Dr. Shulman yet but from what I've heard and read, he's a gentleman."

A disbelieving reporter asked how she would finance her campaign and the young lady replied, "I have a lot of heart. It's not the size of the wallet that counts, you know." The *Telegram* headlined it "Beauty vs. the Beast."

I was delighted with the Liberal choice and offered to campaign together with their candidate at any time.

An amusing offshoot to the contest was the nomination of one Geza Matrai as the candidate of the Edmund Burke society. Matrai produced some colour and heat at the all-candidates meetings with his novel approach to the problems of Communism, homosexuality and welfare – which was to shoot their practitioners. Sadly his campaign came to a sudden end three weeks before the election when Russian premier Kosygin came on a visit to Ottawa and Matrai attempted to attack him. Matrai spent the rest of the election period in jail and didn't even get to vote for himself.

The Tory choice was a different matter. School teacher Yuri Shymko was young, bright and aggressively ethnic. He began hostilities with a lengthy letter to the *Telegram* accusing me of:

- "Materialistic orientation of values" because of my books on finance.
- Blowing the RCMP teenage informant scandal out of proportion.
- Failing to do something about intimidation of Czech refugees via absentee trials taking place in that country.
- Not speaking out on the problems of "intimidation in the Chinese community."

My amusement quickly faded as the Tory campaign unfolded. I was amazed first of all to find I was being used as a bogeyman throughout the province, as insur-

—Star drawing by Fons van Woerkom

ance representative Colin Brown publicly urged every Ontario doctor to donate $50 to either the Tories or the Liberals "to avoid the spectre of Shulman becoming Health Minister." I decided that Mr. Brown was not too well organized when he mailed a copy of his appeal to my medical office.

At the local level, Yuri Shymko began his campaign with an appeal to the various ethnic groups. To the Ukrainians he said, "Vote for one of your own," which was fair enough for he was indeed of Ukrainian origin. But then came the ads on the Polish radio, "Vote Polish. Yuri Shymko's father was Polish." And the ad in the German paper reading, "Vote for your German candidate. Yuri Shymko is a German university professor." Last but not least, was the Maltese pamphlet which read, "Vote Shymko, the only candidate who speaks Maltese." It was all a little too much. That campaign ended suddenly when I read out all of his ads at a public meeting at Humberside Collegiate.

The one burning issue in the riding was the question of financial aid to Catholic high schools, which the Liberals and NDP supported but the Tories opposed. I was astonished to hear Shymko vigorously opposing aid in speeches at the Baptist Church and supporting it the next day at St. Joseph's.

That particular ploy came to an end when I taped his speech to the Catholics and played it to the Baptists.

All of this was perhaps a little seamy but could be understood in the heat of an election. What followed was totally inexcusable and unforgivable, as the Tories attempted to whip up racial hatred.

On Wednesday, September 15, a Conservative worker came to my office and said he was very upset at what was happening at Conservative headquarters. Instructions were being given to all the campaign workers that, in their work in going door-to-door, they were to stress my Communist and Jewish background. I had known this informant for many years as a patient and felt that he was reliable enough to merit checking his story out. I sent in two "volunteers" to Conservative headquarters to see what, in fact, they were saying.

On Wednesday, September 22, these two "volunteers" were instructed to come to a briefing session at the local Conservative headquarters. There were some twenty persons sitting about the room. The campaign manager said, "You are now going to get your campaign instructions. They will be given to you by Miss – who is going to handle this aspect of the campaign." Miss – was introduced. She then said, "We are going to win this campaign. We are going to beat Shulman. By the time this campaign is over, no one will vote for him. We are going to pin the Commie label on him."

She went on to tell them what they were to say door-to-door. She started off with why I was fired as Chief Coroner. Her explanation was that there had been a fire at the Workmen's Compensation Hospital and there were bodies lying everywhere. I was called on a Saturday but didn't show up. They called me again on the Sunday and still I didn't show up. I finally appeared on the Monday with my family and, with the bodies lying all about, held a press conference where my picture was taken for the use of the Toronto papers.

She went on to say, "He is dishonest. He bought stock and didn't pay for it. The police are still trying to get the proof so that they can send him to jail, because they haven't been able to tag him yet. He is a terrible doctor; he is incompetent; he doesn't know what he is doing. He is a bad Jew. He puts up Christmas lights."

Many of the people receiving the Tory instructions came from Eastern European backgrounds and this kind of talk served to whip up the type of racial hatreds which unfortunately are all too familiar in that part of the world. The very next week, two of my workers had their lives threatened. And a brick wrapped with Tory propaganda was thrown through my car window.

On October 6th, a phony pamphlet was distributed through my riding, supposedly from the NDP, which contained material intended to anger uncommitted voters. Among its contents was:

> We recommend the provision to relevant nations, such as some in the Caribbean, of financial aid to enable them to expropriate private Canadian property on their soil.

> Universities – We recommend that tuition fees be abolished to free the student from dependence on his family.

> We recommend the cessation of sales of strategic resources, such as nickel and uranium, to the U.S.A. and governmental allies of the U.S.A., whether in Europe, Asia or Latin America.

Unpleasant incident after incident quickly followed. We found one Conservative campaign worker going door-to-door warning people that, if I was not defeated, the Communists would come to power. One of my supporters, who was also the personnel manager of the Metro Separate School Board, put up my sign in front of his house. Within hours Conservative workers came to his door threatening to beat him up if the sign was not removed immediately. I could hardly blame him for taking it down for as he put it, "I have a family."

In the western, heavily Ukrainian section of the riding, men went door-to-door distributing Conservative literature and telling every home owner, "We have to beat Shulman, the Communist Jew." In the Ukrainian old age home, one of the old ladies made the error of expressing her support for me and was threatened with eviction. My attempt to canvass the patients in the home ended with my being thrown out bodily. On October 12th, the two local Ukrainian newspapers carried a letter saying, "Dr. Shulman came to the Ivan Franco Home on High

Park Gardens and if the NDP is elected the home will be closed and all the old people will be thrown out on the streets." That night, a large black swastika was painted on the side of my office. All over the riding signs suddenly appeared, "Dr. Shulman and the Zionists out." Swastikas also appeared in front of a Polish church where the minister was known to support me. Shops on Roncesvalles Avenue that had put up my signs had bricks thrown through their windows and awnings torn down.

In all my previous political experience I had never run into this type of hatred. In desperation, I finally phoned the Premier, Bill Davis, and begged him to have it stopped. He promised to look into it and, in fact, he did send someone to speak to the Tory office in High Park. But nothing changed. It had been all too easy to whip up the nationalist and anti-semitic sentiments of a small group of right wing Ukrainians but it was not so easy to calm them down again.

I was in a quandary as to how I should run my campaign. Obviously, I was not about to reply with the same type of invective. And I could hardly appeal to voters on the basis of my own ethnic background for there were hardly any Jewish voters in High Park. (In the midst of my troubles I received a letter from the Canadian Jewish Congress demanding that I not appeal for votes on the basis of my Jewish background!) Similarly, I couldn't use the usual NDP campaign approach for the traditional NDP vote was miniscule in West Toronto and the middle-class residents of High Park were not likely to respond favourably to appeals for nationalization or more welfare.

I decided to discard all the material printed up by the central NDP and instead prepared a two-page flyer whose cover read, "What do the Liberals, Conservatives and NDP really think about Morton Shulman?" Inside I placed a series of flattering quotes from people in all three parties, uttered in the Legislature or the press, including the likes of federal NDP leader, Tommy Douglas – "We need more men like him in public life." Liberal MPP Elmer Sopha – "He is what the party over there has needed." And best of all, from Premier John Robarts – "Dr. Shulman is a one-man political party. He has a very definite place in the political spectrum of our country." This approach obviously worked for consternation was reported back from Tory headquarters.

Finally the election came. I had been warned by our infiltrators that some bitter and unhappy Tories planned massive voter impersonations. We countered this by placing people in every poll and first thing election morning we caught one of them red-handed.

High Park is a melange of people from just about every country in Europe and Asia and I had no idea what effect this vicious campaign had had upon them. But I need not have worried. When the election results came in, I found that I had won an overwhelming victory, actually increasing my percentage of the vote from the 49 per cent I won in 1967 to 61 per cent of the total vote. Laima Svegzda came to our headquarters where she gracefully wished me well. The Tory never did concede his defeat.

28 *Wire Taps and Stuffed Ballots*

During the course of the election, reports kept coming in of strange goings-on in the St. Andrews-St. Patrick home riding of Minister Allan Grossman. But I was far too involved in my own problems at the time. After the election, when I did look into it, it became obvious that Grossman had been re-elected only with the help of massive voting fraud (although there was no suggestion that he was personally involved). I took my evidence to the NDP but they did not appear anxious to take any action. Their candidate in the riding, the Rev. Dan Heap (later a Toronto alderman), was quite radical and I had the distinct impression that they did not want him in the caucus.

When the Legislature first met on December 13, 1971, I demanded the floor and presented my evidence:

(1) In eight polls proven impersonations had taken place.

(2) Some persons voted in the advance poll and then again in the regular poll.

(3) In one poll, more votes were cast than there were names on the voters' list.

(4) Eleven polls were visited by two men purporting to represent the returning officer and the scrutineers were ordered to leave while discussions took place with

the deputy returning officer. At one of these polls, when the scrutineers were allowed to re-enter, they noticed the corner of a ballot caught in the edge of the lid where it had not slipped all the way in.

The Tories did not reply to my allegations and, when the Speaker promised to look into them, I demanded an investigation by the Committee on Elections. No investigation ever did take place.

What I didn't know when I made these charges was that three weeks before the election the OPP had placed a tap on the phone of one George B., a local small-time hoodlum, because of suspicion that he was involved in an extortion racket. One week before the election, a startled policeman had heard B. making arrangements to stuff ballots in St. Andrews-St. Patrick, to impersonate voters and to vote in the name of a number of deceased citizens. The police followed B. on election day and saw him, together with five cronies, go from polling booth to polling booth. The day after the election, which the Tories narrowly won in that riding, the police heard B. talking by phone with a senior member of the Tory party and confirming that "the job had been done."

The shocked officers took the tapes to their boss. He told them that he would send them to the Commissioner of the OPP. Later they were told that the Attorney General of the province had ordered that no action be taken. Whether the Attorney General was involved at all or actually heard the tapes we will never know. I did not get the details until much later, and my informant in the OPP made me promise not to raise the matter publicly at that time. But I did send a letter to Premier Bill Davis giving him the details and asking him to take action against the persons involved. He never answered my letter.

29 *The Nutcracker*

Bill Davis did do me one favour in an indirect way. Beginning in 1968, Canada's National Ballet had used various public figures as the stretcher bearers in its annual Christmas production of the Nutcracker Suite. In 1971, their initial choice was Bill Davis but he turned down the honour. I was selected as the second choice. My partner turned out to be Peter Worthington, editor of the Toronto *Sun*.

As dancers, Peter and I were pretty bad. We hammed it up with a little two-step while stars Karen Kain and Frank Augustyn stared in astonishment. As we were being pushed reluctantly off the stage, Peter said to me, "You're a terrible dancer – can you write?" I replied, "I think so." He said, "Come work for me – do a weekly column." I gave a quick "yes" before he could change his mind and on January 11, 1972, I made my debut as a political columnist.

I loved it then! I still do!

There is no greater privilege for a politician than writing a newspaper column and being able to present issues as he sees them. For years I had worked my guts out on various problems and injustices, some of which impressed the newspapers and received great publicity and some of which were ignored completely. All too often a story

would begin, "Minister A. today denied Morton Shulman's charge that . . ." and I would find myself shot
down on the basis of one tiny aspect of a huge story that
received no other coverage. On the other hand, I was
determined not to get myself into a conflict-of-interest
situation or be accused of using the column to advance
my own electoral prospects. I solved this quickly by announcing that I would not run at the next election. This
decision was quite simple in the light of my continuing
feud with NDP leader Stephen Lewis who had made it
quite clear that I had no bright future while he led the
party.

I found that a newspaper column was even more effective than pressure from the Legislature in redressing
injustice. My first column on January 11, 1972 read:

> Charles Dyer is 72 and an old North Bay railroad man.
> Twenty-two years ago in 1950 he purchased a health and
> accident policy from the Mutual Benefit Health and
> Accident Association, now known as Mutual of Omaha.
> In 1959, Dyer became ill with a blockage of the blood
> vessels to his legs which gradually cost him his ability to
> walk more than a few steps. He has not worked since
> then and is now unable to leave his home for any pur-
> pose.
>
> For eleven years Mutual of Omaha paid Dyer the $80
> monthly required by the policy. But on February 23,
> 1970 payments were discontinued because on Page 2 of
> Charles Dyer's policy it states that benefits will be paid
> for disability "which confines the insured continuously
> within doors and requires regular visits therein by a
> legally qualified physician or surgeon."
>
> Even the insurance company doesn't suggest that Dyer
> has ever been able to return to work, but they point out
> quite accurately that he obviously was not continuously
> confined within doors if he was able to go to see his doc-
> tor at his office to have the insurance forms filled out
> instead of having the doctor visit him. (Unfortunately
> the doctor doesn't make house calls.) They back up their

argument by quoting the doctor who wrote them on April 14, 1970: "Although over the years I have never advised him to remain indoors, he now tells me that he does so. He states that, except for coming to my office, he remains at home as he finds it too difficult to walk outside."

Meanwhile, Charles Dyer has lost the last use of his legs and is no longer able to leave his home even for medical treatment. Fortunately he has found another physician who does make house calls.

I don't really expect much from insurance companies, for, regardless of their fancy pledges, they are really in business for the purpose of making money. Now the last hope in the Charles Dyer case rests with the new Minister of Commercial and Financial Affairs, Gordon Carton. I shall let you know his response.

Prior to writing the column I had appealed fruitlessly to the insurance company and the government on Mr. Dyer's behalf and had been rebuffed. But within days of my debut as a writer, Mutual of Omaha received a phone call from the new provincial Minister of Public Protection, my old antagonist Eric Winkler, and just one week later Charles Dyer received a cheque from the insurance company for all the monies owed him dating back to October 5, 1970.

I learned my lesson well and I have used the column ever since to fight injustice and stand up for the rights of the powerless. I think I've been quite successful at it. The *Sun* pays me $150 per week but I enjoy it so much that I often think I should pay them for the privilege of writing it.

In the Legislature my life continued much as before. I let the NDP go their own way in their pursuits of more welfare and higher taxes while I kept up my own private war with the Tories who, in their zeal for private enterprise, were allowing many a shady deal to flourish in Ontario.

In February 1972, I delivered an attack on the relatively inactive Department of Consumer Protection
which had done nothing to protect buyers of worthless
scrub in Northern Ontario. A firm called Reid and Zalsman was running ads all over the U.S.A. offering northern
bush as "an investment where you can't lose." The ads
described the land as a sportsman's paradise and mentioned that "the large metropolitan area of Toronto,
population about two million, is to the south." They
didn't mention that Toronto was almost four hundred
miles to the south.

I sent one of my employees to the Reid and Zalsman
offices pretending to be a prospective purchaser and the
lady was offered eighty-five acres, twelve miles north of
Englehart, for $3,695. I phoned a real estate agent in
the area who told me that the land had no resale value.
"There is ice till May, the black flies come in June, the
mosquitoes arrive in July and freeze-up is November 1.
Anyway, there are no roads so the only way into the
property is by parachute!" The ad's description of the
property was a little different: "It is in the world-
famous Larder Lake mining district, where fortunes
have been made, and can be made in the future. If you
purchase this property your future nest egg may be
there."

A swamp near Rainy River was advertised for $3,695
as

> . . . a rare find located just four miles from the world-
> famous Lake of the Woods. It has a road several hundred
> yards to the south which connects with Highway 600 to
> the east of the acreage. Rainy River town can be reached
> to the south about ten miles.
>
> Large Lake of the Woods to the west is truly a magnifi-
> cent lake, about sixty-four miles across from north to
> south and nearly as wide in an east and west direction. It
> would require a lifetime to explore its innumerable bays
> and the passages among its 16,000 islands. It will always

remain a happy hunting ground for the nature lovers of the world.

Forty-pound lunge are caught and this lake boasts a world's record for this fish. Great Northern pike, salmon pike, walleyed pike, black bass and nearly all other fresh water fish are found in abundance.

There are still large stands of timber sheltering game in abundance: deer, bear, wildfowl in season, beaver and other wildlife.

Supplies and services would be obtained at the town of Rainy River where there is a border crossing point connecting with Baudette, Minnesota.

I asked the clerk of the local township if there would be enough dry land to build a house on the property to which he replied laughing, "There might be room to plant a flagpole on a outcropping of rock."

I soon learned that the same lands had been sold again and again. For as soon as the disappointed American purchasers attempted to visit "their land" and learned they had been taken, they would stop paying taxes and lose the title.

Oddly enough, the provincial government went to great efforts to protect Ontario purchasers of land *outside* of Ontario, even going so far as to send inspectors as far as Spain to make sure that advertised properties were as represented. Their excuse for not protecting American purchasers of worthless Ontario bush was a loophole in the law which read, "No person shall in any capacity, trade in real estate where the real estate is a lot or unit of land in a subdivision *located outside Ontario* until there has been filed with the registrar a prospectus containing the prescribed information and until there has been obtained from the registrar a certificate of acceptance thereof."

I tried to remove this excuse for inaction by bringing

in a private member's bill which would have deleted the phrase, "located outside Ontario," from the legislation but the government refused to allow its passage. Northern Affairs Minister Leo Bernier said, "There's nothing that they're doing that contravenes any laws."

My efforts were all in vain. The law never was changed and the sales are going on to this day.

30 *Gordon Carton*

While most of the cabinet rejected any of my suggestions out of hand, there were several cabinet ministers with whom I had excellent personal relationships and who were always ready to take a fair look at any problem. These included Fern Guindon, Syl Apps, Dick Potter and Gordon Carton. Carton never took on the biased, one-sided "me good, you bad" attitude of so many of his colleagues and I always found it a great pleasure to work with him.

Just prior to the 1971 election, a small manufacturing firm in the centre of my riding was struck by the local union seeking more money and better working conditions. The owner of the company was an immigrant who had built up his business from nothing, knew all of his workers personally and took their strike as a personal slight. He swore that he would never give in and hired a company of strikebreakers called Canadian Driver Pool. They sent in workers and guards and over a period of several weeks gradually restored the plant to its full production.

The men on the picket line slowly ran out of money as did their small union and finally they came to me in desperation as they realized the strike was lost. One week before election day, I went to the company and pleaded with – no, begged – the owner to settle the strike and take the men back. I warned him, "There is just an outside chance the NDP might win this election and, if they do, people like yourself are going to be in trouble." He smiled and said, "Let's wait for a few days." And the day after the election he sent me a message saying that the strikers would stay out forever.

I went to see Gordon Carton, then Minister of Labour, and told him the whole story, asking him to intervene as a personal favour to me. The next day Carton phoned me to say, "Tomorrow the company will make an offer to the union. For goodness sake, make sure they don't haggle on it."

I phoned the union leader. "You are going to get a decent offer. Don't try to change a comma. Grab it because the company would like you to reject it or to haggle so they can turn it down."

The offer came through and it was a good one. Everyone was hired back with a decent raise and with no reprisals. The men were grateful, the union enormously relieved and I became a permanent Gordon Carton fan. In a better government all this might be routine for a Minister of Labour, but Ontario has seen few of his ilk. I am sorry that Carton did not remain in politics but Premier Davis transferred him shortly afterwards to the Ministry of Transportation where his main job was to defend the government's cancellation of the Spadina Expressway. Carton believed this was a wrong decision and he retired soon after. Shortly before his retirement he said bitterly to me, "At least you in the opposition can say what you believe."

In the brief time that he was Minister of Transport, even Gordon Carton proved that being a Tory minister can produce a blindness to justice in the best willed of men. It came about because of the widening of Highway 550 near Sault Ste. Marie. Representatives of the Department of Highways called on a Mr. and Mrs. Charles

James and told them that they needed the front twenty-nine feet of their property in order to widen the highway.

Mr. James was very upset because that would mean losing all the old trees across a 331 foot frontage and the removal of these trees, which gave charm and privacy to the property, would leave the area completely flat and barren.

Mr. James suggested that the curve of the road could be pulled in a little and land taken from the other side, from the undeveloped backs of other properties, which would involve going back no more than ten feet in depth.

But the Highway Department people were not willing to consider this. However, they said that if Mr. and Mrs. James did not agree to the settlement, they would issue an expropriation order. They offered to pay five cents per square foot for the land or a total of $375 for the 6,447 square feet that was to be expropriated.

Under Ontario law, the government cannot expropriate land over an owner's objection until after an inquiry has been held, and Mrs. James demanded that such an inquiry be held. After a few weeks she received a notice that such an inquiry was to be held and that the Department of Transport had itself appointed the inquiry officer!

In the weeks before the hearing, Mrs. James made repeated requests to the department for information which they were required to provide under the act "at least five days before the hearing," giving the facts on which they based their claim that the expropriation was necessary. Mrs. James was put off repeatedly and the information was not put into her hands until she was actually in the chamber and the hearing was about to begin.

Mrs. James did not engage counsel and spoke for herself while the Department of Transport was represented by counsel and a battery of engineers and experts. To the surprise of all, inquiry officer John H. McDonald, QC, found that Mrs. James was right and "that the suggested expropriation is not really necessary."

Immediately following this announcement, the Minister of Transport expropriated the James property!

When I raised this matter in the Legislature with the normally sensible Transport Minister, he pointed out that the letter of the law had been followed. It was true that the expropriation act required that an inquiry be held when a citizen objected to his land being expropriated. But, the act did not require that the department pay any heed to the results of the inquiry!

He went on to say that the decision to expropriate had been made by his predecessor, Charles McNaughton, but that he had personally looked it over and agreed with it.

This decision was doubly astounding and depressing coming from Gordon Carton who represented the bright side of Bill Davis' usually obdurate cabinet. It spurred me on to renewed battle against the Tories.

31 *Crooked Unions*

In my investigations into organized crime I had run into evidence indicating that a number of labour unions were corrupt. This posed a special problem to me as a representative of the NDP, the party partially supported and financed by labour. There was never any question in my mind that the crooks had to be exposed in the unions just as anywhere else. But I had some doubt as to how this would be received by my colleagues. In January 1972, my doubts were laid at rest when I put the evidence before Stephen Lewis. He didn't hesitate in telling me to go right ahead, and on March 10, 1972 I presented the facts to the Legislature.

In one union, the International Brotherhood of Boilermakers, a whole series of incredible events had taken place.

• The trustees of the union had discovered that the treasury had been looted. They called in an accountant, one Sydney Posner, who discovered that wages were being understated in an effort to swindle the tax authorities. The trustees complained to their headquarters in the U.S. but were ignored.

• Some of the $150 initiation fees never reached the treasury but were pocketed by union officials.

• $23,000 in government bonds mysteriously disappeared. When the union discovered that I was investigating their disappearance, they reappeared just as mysteriously.

• One employee was listed as being paid and the money went somewhere but, in fact, the employee had left months before.

• Officials of the union used union funds to pay for hundreds of dollars of parking tickets and other personal expenses.

• Workers were not allowed to vote on collective agreements.

• Members were not allowed to vote on the rebates of their health plan. When they objected they were told it was "too complicated for them to understand."

• When the union trustees laid official charges with the international union that their treasury had been looted, these charges were dismissed on the grounds that they were "not timely," whatever that meant.

Incidentally, that same union sent a letter to their hiring halls giving a list of men who were not to be hired in the future either because they were Communists or trouble-makers or "had been involved in strikes!"

In another union, the plasterers, part of the pay was in the form of stamps worth $2.05 per hour which were to be refunded by the union to the workers. Many of them had over $1,000 due. But when they attempted to get their money, they were threatened and ordered from the union offices. Appeals to the Ontario Department of Labour were ignored and the men finally came to me in the hope that public exposure would embarrass the union into paying them or the government into taking action.

The plasterers' union's response to my broadside was relatively mild. They announced that they were referring the matter to their solicitor David Lewis, national leader of the NDP. Lewis promptly stated that he was no longer their solicitor and that he wanted nothing to do with the matter. Amazingly, the whole matter seemed to die there, at least publicly. In actual fact, I learned later that the Department of Labour and the leaders of the larger international unions were appalled and had put pressure on both craft unions to clean house or face government intervention. Within weeks the money owed to the plasterers had been paid and the local crooks in the boilermakers' union were eased out to "retirement."

I thought that my battle with crooked unions was over. But I couldn't have been more wrong.

32 Defeats

While this battle was going on I ran into a series of small defeats; small, that is, in the over-all picture, but still important and tragic to the people involved.

The Leonard Prior case was a source of great frustration to me. Fifty-year-old Prior had purchased a tourist camp in 1956 on Whiskey Lake, part of the Serpent Lake system, and had gradually built up a respectable business. But he had one continuing worry due to rumours of pollution of the water system from the uranium mines upstream. Before he bought the camp, Prior had checked with the Ontario Department of Lands and Forests who had reassured him saying, "Strict control of neutralization of all acid wastes will be maintained and it is not expected that there will be any adverse effect on Whiskey Lake or the Serpent River watershed . . . . Neither standard water analysis nor the very sensitive spectroanalysis have revealed any substances which would be harmful to fish or aquatic life . . . . The industries have co-operated excellently and have assured the department that they will undertake whatever measures that may be necessary to protect the quality of the waters receiving mining wastes."

So assured, Mr. and Mrs. Prior purchased the lodge and worked hard to build it up. By 1964 they had done so well that they were able to expand and build a new cottage and they planned to build more cottages the following spring. But then disaster struck in the form of an announcement from the Ontario Water Resources Commission that the Serpent River watershed was polluted both chemically and radioactively. The announcement was followed by the death of all the fish in Whiskey Lake and then by a further announcement that the water was not safe to drink.

Needless to say, tourists do not go to fishing lodges where there are no fish and where the water is polluted. Leonard Prior's business quickly decayed and his earnings gradually disappeared.

When the Priors sought financial damages from the mining companies, they were told they could not collect for their business failure because Rio Algom and Denison were not legally responsible.

Leonard Prior struggled to keep his lodge going, encouraging his guests to portage to other lakes. But it was a hopeless battle and gradually his guests stopped coming. By 1969 he was broke.

Now began for the Priors a three-year struggle. They wrote to various government officials seeking help to relocate on the basis of the government's 1956 assurances, but no one was willing to help. The then Minister of Northern Affairs, Al Lawrence, told them that, "The Mining Act of Ontario does not have a section requiring compensation by the mining companies for an injured person." John Robarts wrote that, "I regret there is no provincial program under which assistance could be provided." René Brunelle, the Minister of Lands and Forests, said he was sorry he couldn't help. The Northern Ontario Development Corporation said, "We are sorry to tell you that there are no N.O.D.C. programs through which we could assist you."

Finally, Leonard Prior appealed to the Prime Minister of the province, Bill Davis, who replied that he would not help and went on, "I cannot agree that this problem was caused by government negligence, because there was no way of knowing that tailings disposal from the mines would eventually result in radiological pollution of the watershed . . . I regret that I cannot be of more assistance to you."

I raised hell with the government in the Legislature and received promises that they would look into it. But nothing was ever done.

I did no better with a bad situation in the Department of Public Works. For the preceding twenty years the provincial government had hired most of its maintenance workers on a "temporary" basis. Actually, they worked full time year after year. Because they were "temporary" workers, they received somewhat higher pay than the regular civil service but they did not get any of the extras the regular employees received, that is, there was no vacation pay, sick pay or job security.

Suddenly the government decided that these hundreds of employees should be taken into the civil service and made "permanent." This was fine except that they were to receive up to a 45 per cent drop in pay. Men who had been earning $240 a week were to be dropped to $125 a week. Needless to say, the employees were appalled and came to me asking for help. Before coming to me they had been to their boss in the department to beg for help, complaining that they would not be able to keep up the payments on their homes with such a massive reduction in earnings.

One of the men had pleaded, "I am sixty years of age. I've been earning $5.65 an hour, how can I now manage on $3.06 an hour? I have five children." And the official replied in front of all the witnesses, "Who told you to have five children?"

I did everything possible, including a personal appeal to Bill Davis, but it was all in vain. The cuts went through as planned.

I also had no luck with the case of policeman Gordon Smyth of the little town of St. Mary's. Smyth's ordeal had begun the previous summer. He was listed to take his vacation from August 14 to August 30 but, during that time, two of his cases were due to come up in court, one involving a case that had originated eighteen months earlier, the second a preliminary hearing involving a man charged with possession of burglary tools.

Smyth tried to have the dates of the trials changed so that they would not fall within his vacation period but was told that this was not possible. He then approached the Chief of Police and asked if he could change the dates of his vacation. The Chief said this was not possible since he (the Chief) had to attend a course at the Ontario Police College. Since nothing could be done about it, Smyth went off on his vacation, promising to return for the two court appearances.

The Smyth family took a tent trailer and camped on Bass Lake near Wiarton and on August 17 he drove back and appeared in court uneventfully. On August 23 he again came back from his vacation and made the required court appearance but this time disaster took place in a most unexpected form.

Under court rules, witnesses are allowed mileage fees of ten cents per mile and Constable Smyth entered a claim for 398 miles. The mileage resulted from Smyth's visit to Tobermory on August 21 to visit a friend. When the Smyth family arrived in Tobermory, they found that the friend was at a lighthouse on an island north of Tobermory. So the Smyths decided to stay overnight in Tobermory and the next morning returned to Bass Lake where the constable picked up his evidence notebook and drove off to court in Stratford.

On September 24, the Chief called Smyth into his office and asked him about the bill rendered for the 398 miles. Subsequently, Smyth was accused of never having been to Tobermory and so of having rendered a mileage bill some $20.70 higher than it should have been. There now ensued an incredible series of events.

The police commission of St. Mary's held a closed disciplinary hearing after which they offered Smyth two alternatives: (1) Resignation within seven days and "all evidence, transcripts etc. that pertained to this case will be destroyed, so that no record will be on file in the municipality and no statement will be issued to the press and the matter will be forgotten." (2) Immediate dismissal.

Was Smyth really in Tobermory? St. Mary's police officer Don Bartalacci had gone to Bass Lake on the weekend before August 23 and found that Smyth was not there. His trailer was occupied by Smyth's son-in-law who said Smyth had gone to Tobermory.

When Smyth was asked to produce some proof he was at Tobermory, he told of visiting a fishery where his children were weighed on a fishery scale. He also described one of the men there with whom he had a discussion. The police commission did not even bother to visit the fishery and check his story. I couldn't believe that such a penalty could be justified even if he had been guilty. Once again I appealed to the Legislature for justice. Once again my plea was rejected.

There was a similarly frustrating lack of action when I discovered that the new OHIP scheme was being milked by non-medical personnel. The government paid on a fee-for-service basis and some chiropodists had discovered that they could make a fortune by going into nursing homes and making the rounds of all the patients. One man was collecting $300 an hour for clipping toe nails. Once again there were big headlines. Once again nothing came of it.

A few unscrupulous doctors were just as bad. A worker at OHIP leaked me documents showing a multi-million dollar rip-off of the public insurance scheme. Doctors were billing OHIP for seeing up to 155 patients per day;

one psychiatrist held group sessions and billed for the patients individually and many doctors on hospital staffs were rendering bills for patients treated by their interns who they had never seen. All this in addition to the continuing rip-off involving medical labs and the referring for lab work of patients to the doctors' own labs.

The publicity that followed my public release of the documents did some good. A number of doctors were reprimanded or disciplined by the College of Physicians

and $50,000 was recovered from a few worried physicians. But, as I have already pointed out, the abuse in medical labs never was corrected. My informant estimated that in 1972 the province was losing one million dollars a month for non-rendered medical services.

The response of organized medicine to my disclosures startled me. The president of the Ontario Medical Association, Dr. L. R. Harnick, accused me of showing contempt for the judicial process and of denying doctors basic justice. Dr. Harnick said my press conference was ill-advised, because I had disclosed evidence in cases already being investigated by the College of Physicians and Surgeons. Dr. Harnick concluded by attacking my personal medical practice: "If Dr. Shulman is practising seven hours a day, he obviously is not spending as much time in the Legislative Assembly as his electors have a right to expect. As a self-confessed millionaire with a net income from his part-time medical practice of $32,000 plus the $18,000 he receives from the public purse ($6,000 of which is tax free) as a part-time member of the Legislature, Dr. Shulman is in a poor position to question the income of full-time doctors who work sixty to seventy hours a week providing excellent service to their patients."

Somehow I got the impression that the medical profession was not grateful for my efforts.

33 *The Silver Mine that Wasn't*

In April 1972 I became involved in one of the more bizarre episodes of my political career. It all began when I received a complaint from a shareholder of a defunct silver company, Glen Lake Silver, that the shareholders had been robbed of their equity and that, after this was done, the provincial government helped to finance and promote a new company with their assets.

The facts were these: Glen Lake Silver had run out of ore two years earlier at its Cobalt silver mine and had paid out all its cash assets in dividends but still owned the exhausted mine together with a complete set of mining machinery on the property. Through a complex series of financial transactions, the crooked promoters running the company had put Glen Lake into bankruptcy by loaning it $700,000, siphoning off the money and then foreclosing on the company ninety days later when Glen Lake couldn't make the interest payments on the $700,000.

The assets of Glen Lake were then put up for public auction. There were a number of bidders between $50,000 and $100,000 but the original promoters bid $700,000 and purchased the assets. Actually, they were bidding with non-existent money for they immediately paid the $700,000 back to themselves to satisfy the original $700,000 loan.

The result of all this was that the shareholders of Glen Lake were told that their company had gone bankrupt. The property was taken over by the original promoters who promptly sold it to a company called International Mariner, run by Toronto stock promoter Norty Cooper. Cooper set up a subsidiary of International Mariner called Silver Shield specifically to run the old Glen Lake property, issued stock to the public and began a massive promotion campaign.

Cooper was indeed unique. A New York public relations firm he hired described him as a "Canadian maverick, flamboyant, energetic and totally committed to anything he does." His life style "at work and play is in the realm of many of the world's business moguls we read about. His 500-acre showplace ranch in Florida, where he breeds horses and Angus cattle and himself oversees every bucket of oats, boasts America's largest private swimming pool and two saunas and is a fitting compliment to his business life style. His magnificent offices in Toronto are complete with closed-circuit television, electronic doors and a row of buttons that connects him immediately with brokers, bankers, lawyers, etc." He and Silver Shield now are taking "rather exciting steps to revive the silver industry in Canada and to provide Canadians (and the world) with the first silver industrial complex in the world."

In this campaign, Cooper was vigorously helped by the provincial government. They began by giving him $37,500 for exploration and the deputy minister of the Department of National Resources together with Alan Eagleson, the president of the Ontario Progressive Conservative Association, personally went with Cooper on a promotional trip to Cobalt where Cooper announced plans for development of the mine and construction of both a silver refinery and a mint!

Cobalt is a very depressed town in Northern Ontario and, if the refinery had actually been built, it would have been a tremendous boost to the area. On that basis, Cooper approached the federal Department of Regional Economic Expansion who pledged $750,000 towards the project. To their later dismay, both Ontario's Minister of Natural Resources, Leo Bernier, and the up-and-coming Liberal politician, John Roberts, were quoted in the press as heartily congratulating Cooper on the project.

Cooper's appeal was amazingly simple – he called it "vertical integration." "Instead of mining silver in Northern Ontario and shipping it south for refining and then sending the refined ore to a mint in the U.S., we'll do it all in Cobalt. It makes sense – it saves money and we will be a great success." .

I think Norty Cooper really believed every word he said – he had fallen in love with his own deal. But the facts were that the very same mine had closed just two years earlier for lack of silver ore and a refinery in Cobalt had closed just the year before because there was not enough silver in the area to keep it going. To this day I don't know why all the politicians had not realized this before getting involved. One other fact they apparently had not noticed was that Silver Shield was paying $279,000 a year to Cooper for "management and administrative services."

On May 8, 1972 I took the story to the Legislature. My facts were not welcomed. Minister of Natural Resources Leo Bernier replied to my demands for an investigation: "Mr. Chairman, I don't have any machinery within my department to conduct an investigation which is what the member is really calling for. I think this is the responsibility of some other ministry within this government. If he wants to level any accusations, any statements of fraud or misappropriation of public funds he should direct his comments to the federal government – whose $750,000 is going to the proposal in which he is so vitally interested and concerned – and not this government."

The Tory member for the area, Ed Havrot, was furious. He insisted that he had looked into the facts and supported the Silver Shield project. He warned me that if I came to Cobalt I would be skinned alive! It wasn't only the politicians who couldn't see. The Kirkland Lake *Northern News* wrote a full-page editorial which concluded, "It seems the 300 miles distance between the Ontario Legislature and Cobalt appears to have somewhat fogged Mr. Shulman's view of a project that promises to show a bright future for both the new company and the town of Cobalt."

Norty Cooper responded to my attacks with complete insouciance, insisted the project was viable and the next day invited me to come to Silver Shield with a mining engineer of my choice and see it for myself. I made haste to accept and chose as my companion independent engineer and millionaire Pat Sheridan. Cooper certainly did have style – he flew us to Cobalt in a private plane and laid on a grand tour of the mine and the area. I couldn't tell a silver mine from any other hole in the ground but Sheridan emerged to write a devastating report.

He said that Silver Shield was a "small, typical Cobalt operation" with enough ore to operate profitably for about a year. He pointed out that the ore would run out before the refinery could be completed and that "the entire theory of vertical integration suffers from the extremely short proven life of the mine."

Now everything quickly fell apart. First of all, two federal employees who had recommended the grant to Silver Shield were suspended from their jobs "in connection with purchases of shares of Silver Shield." This was followed by withdrawal of the federal grant and a collapse in the price of shares of Silver Shield. Then the company declared bankruptcy, the refinery was cancelled and the mine sold. Finally Norton Cooper was charged with "extending a benefit" to a federal official and ended up in jail.

At Queen's Park, the Tory officials were totally un-repentant and insisted that, if I had just not stirred things up, everything would have worked out!

34 *Phony Votes*

My aggravation with the phony votes held in the Legislature came to a boil at the beginning of June 1972 when I had a row with the Chairman of the House. It had all started several weeks before when Minister of Commercial and Financial Affairs Eric Winkler announced with a great flourish and much publicity that he was bringing in legislation which would prevent U.S. takeovers of brokers and other middlemen in the Ontario insurance industry. When the legislation actually arrived in the House on May 16, what it actually said was that no U.S. citizen or corporation could own more than half of the issued shares of a company in the insurance field. Since control of any publicly held stock can be achieved with far less than fifty per cent of the issued stock, the new law was, in effect, meaningless.

The Opposition members of the Legislature at first presumed that this was a simple error as the result of Winkler's ignorance of this subject. And so the knowledgeable NDP and Liberal members slowly and patiently explained the flaw in the law to him. They began to become upset when, after it had been explained, he still refused to make the necessary changes in the legislation, offering no reason for his refusal.

It now became apparent to everyone in the House that the legislation had simply been a public relations ploy and that the government had no intention of preventing U.S. takeovers in the industry. When the vote on the bill was taken at 9:30 PM, fifteen Liberal and NDP members supported an amendment that would have put teeth into the bill, while twelve Conservatives supported the government's untenable position.

To our absolute astonishment, the Chairman of the House, Mr. Russell Rowe, said that the Conservatives had won the vote. I exploded and raged and pounded my desk with fury. Hansard records it as follows:

Mr. Chairman:	In my opinion, the "nays" have it.
Mr. Shulman:	Mr. Chairman, on a point of order, we outnumber them. You can't count, you have deliberately misled everyone.

Interjections by Hon. Members.

Mr. Shulman:	Can't you count?
Mr. Chairman:	Order, please. Order, please.
Mr. Shulman:	You can't count. We won that vote.
Mr. Chairman:	Order, please. The Hon. Member must know the Chairman doesn't have to count.
Mr. Shulman:	He can't listen either. He has no eyes, he has no ears, he has no sense.

Interjections by Hon. Members.

Mr. Chairman:	Order, please! May I point out to the Hon. Member something I shouldn't have to point out. The Chairman is not called upon to count the people here, he cannot assume which way the people will

	vote in any party, so we can only go by the voice and the voice was as evenly split as possible and I was sitting in the middle of it right here. That is right.
Mr. Shulman:	You have made my point. If the voices were evenly split how did you come to the decision that the amendment had not carried?
Mr. Chairman:	There is a very well established rule in all rules of parliamentary procedure that the Chairman is entitled to rule in the direction in which the anticipated vote will go, or is anticipated to go. This is very firmly established.

I found what Mr. Rowe had said almost unbelievable. For, in effect, this meant that it was irrelevant how many members were in the House to vote, but that the government would win every vote, whether their members were present or not.

Russell Rowe had a very strange view of the meaning of parliamentary democracy!

Perhaps equally strange is that with the Tories' huge majority they couldn't persuade more than twelve of their seventy-eight members to remain in the House while important bills were being debated and voted upon. But then, if the Tories controlled the Chair, they didn't *need* to have a majority.

35 *Allan Grossman*

In 1972 my old antagonist Allan Grossman was transferred to the post of Minister of Revenue. We continued our running battle but I had no more success than before.

A Toronto lawyer had come to me complaining that he had written the Department of Revenue asking whether the sales tax had been paid on a transaction involving the purchase of a truck. The department at first wrote him back saying they "understood" that it had. Then two weeks later they wrote again saying they did not have anyone available to check whether the tax had been paid. Then, finally, they wrote again two weeks after that saying they had checked but it was a secret and they would not tell the lawyer.

In the Legislature I asked Grossman if this type of information was available to the public:

Mr. Shulman:	If I am rather dubious and I want to be sure it is paid (the sales tax) who should I write to in your department?
Hon. Mr. Grossman:	Retail Sales Branch.
Mr. Shulman:	Retail Sales Branch and, of course, they would be able to look it up and let me know, is that the situation?

Hon. Mr. Grossman:	Yes.
Mr. Shulman:	Leaving this case aside for the moment, can the Minister tell me what is the policy in relation to requests of this nature to find out whether retail sales tax has been paid?
Hon. Mr. Grossman:	It is not the policy of the department to advise, to let people know, about the situation as to whether someone else has paid a tax or not.

I mulled that one over and could not quite figure out what Grossman had meant, so I tried again in the Legislature the next day:

Mr. Shulman:	Can the Minister explain the minor discrepancy in his two statements made in the last twenty-four hours, in one of which he said that information about payments of retail sales tax were available to the public and in the second of which he said such information was not available to the public.
Hon. Mr. Grossman:	Of course, Mr. Speaker, that is a contradiction ... I should not have said yes to the whole question. I should have said yes – write to the Retail Sales Tax but you won't get the answer as to whether he's paid his sales tax or not.

Perhaps for the first time in my career, I was left speechless!

36 *Life Insurance*

Purely by chance I now stumbled into what should have been a very important issue but which eventually fizzled out. I had always believed that life insurance was very straightforward and that it didn't really matter which company you patronized. But as a result of a tip from an insurance company executive, I did an analysis of the charges by different companies and found that the same policy could vary greatly in cost depending on where you bought it.

I obtained a copy of the statistical tables published annually by the firm of Stone and Cox and, in the summer of 1972, I distributed a breakdown of the true costs of life insurance from the different companies. The figures were startling and they certainly upset the insurance industry. For example, the true cost of a twenty year pay life policy of $10,000 purchased at the age of thirty-five was $84.30 per year from Montreal Life, $37.60 from Metropolitan Life, $17.30 from London Life and $4.90 from North American Life, while the same policy, if purchased from Mutual of Canada, would have ended up costing nothing for that company had paid out $12.20 more in dividends than it received in premiums. I was surprised that the more competitive companies had not publicized these figures previously and I never was able to find out why they had not.

Allan Lingard, the executive director of the Life Under-
writers' Association of Canada, replied that while he was
sure that there were differences in the final cost of
policies from company to company, he felt that the
public was adequately informed of these differences. He
said that Stone and Cox's book is available in every public library and the federal Superintendent of Insurance
publishes a blue book giving detailed information about
companies. "I think there is adequate disclosure," he
concluded. Eric Winkler, Minister of Public Protection,
responded that "reviewing insurance company rates is a
complex thing" but that he was considering making public comparisons of the costs of insurance policies.

Winkler never did get around to it but for the next
four years I issued my annual report on the true cost of
life insurance which received wide publicity across the
country and which, I think, was responsible for many
persons' decisions on where to buy. Unfortunately, when
I retired from politics in 1975, no one thought it worth-
while to continue that work.

This would not be my only involvement with the mysterious ways of the life insurance business. In February
1972, a card was dropped in the mailbox of Edgar Swift
in Campbellford offering to sell mortgage insurance
policies at reasonable prices. As a result, on March 30,
1972, an agent for Occidental Life of California wrote
up a $10,000 life insurance policy for Mr. Swift. Swift
made out a cheque for the first month's payment to
Occidental and the agent informed him that the insurance was effective immediately.

Occidental cashed the cheque and instructed Swift to
go to see their doctor for a medical and to the local
hospital for a chest X-ray. Mr. Swift complied and, as far
as he knew, there was no problem and he believed that
he was now covered by the insurance.

On June 25, 1972, Edgar Swift was killed in a car
accident. On June 26, 1972, Occidental cancelled his

insurance saying, "We appreciate this opportunity to serve you. However, we have not received everything necessary to complete the application. Since no insurance can be provided because of this, any payment you have made will be returned to you in exchange for the receipt given to you."

Mr. Swift's widow appealed to the company to reconsider their harsh decision and the company's Canadian representative referred her plea to the head office in Los Angeles which wrote to Mrs. Swift as follows:

> Mr. Swift applied for insurance on March 30, 1972, and our Conditional Receipt was given to him. This receipt specifies that it provides no insurance until all its conditions are met. One of the conditions is that the policy must be issued at the class of risk applied for. In his application, Mr. Swift applied at the Standard Class of Premium. Based on the medical history he gave us regarding the surgery in 1970 for the duodenal ulcer, we were unable to approve a policy at standard rates. Although we did request, in addition to the medical exam, an X-ray, the substandard rating is based solely on the ulcer history.
>
> Since the conditions of the conditional receipt were not satisfied, no insurance could have been effective until the additional substandard premium was paid and the policy was delivered to Mr. Swift during his life and continued insurability.

Mrs. Swift now appealed to me and I wrote to John Clement, the Minister of Consumer Relations. Clement referred the matter to the Superintendent of Insurance and then wrote back that he was very sorry that he could not help – for, after all, the insurance company had acted entirely within their legal rights.

As a last resort, I called Mr. Addie, the local Vice-President of Occidental who said, "We have made full and complete disclosure to the Department of Insurance – there is nothing more I can add."

I wrote the case up in the *Sun* and raised hell about it in the Legislature. As a result, Occidental received dozens of letters from worried policy holders. The company responded with a letter signed by one Reuben Schafer sent to the *Sun*:

> Occidental did not cancel Swift's insurance after he died simply because it was never able to issue a policy for him! The June 26 letter mailed to him specifying "no insurance can be provided" is known as the "Incomplete Papers Letter," a letter which is mailed to the applicant only after Occidental's file has been closed, because the applicant has not supplied the company with all the information its underwriting department requires to be able to reach a decision whether or not it can issue a policy.
>
> In this case, the file was closed by Occidental at least two weeks before Mr. Swift died.
>
> Dr. Shulman omitted two very important sentences when he quoted the Incomplete Papers Letter in his column. These sentences were: "Your Occidental representative has details of the information needed" and "if the information is furnished, we will re-open consideration of your application for insurance."
>
> Obviously, Occidental's hands were tied, but it was quite willing to consider issuing a policy for Mr. Swift once he submitted the required information.
>
> Shulman has been extremely unfair. Phrases such as "harsh decision" and "cruel behaviour" are emotionally laden and totally uncalled for. It's regrettable that he would play on people's emotions in this sad case by distorting the facts.
>
> If newspapers could exert the same control over their contributors as they do over their reporters, this column never could have appeared.

I responded by blasting the insurance company once again in the *Sun*:

This insurance company seems to think that it absolves them of responsibility by writing to a man already dead, offering to return his premium and telling him to talk to his agent and submit more information. It does not appear to have entered their corporate heads that it is too late to take action like this after their client has been killed – at least morally if not legally.

I had hoped by writing that column that it might produce someone at Occidental who would step in to help the widow. It turned out to be a vain hope.

That did it. On June 12th, 1973, the insurance company gave in and paid the $10,000. Howard Baker, U.S. manager of Occidental's Claims Division said that it had been an executive committee decision to pay the claim. He said that he had received a telephone call from the Toronto office about the bad publicity the case had received and their "inability to convince anybody that the lady should not be paid."

No case ever gave me more satisfaction.

37 The Attorney General Wasn't There

I had by now compiled a new mass of information on organized crime and was about to unload it on the Legislature. I began by questioning the government as to why no action had been taken against the persons involved in the various cases. Invariably the government ministers refused to answer, saying it was not in the public interest. From there, they proceeded to absurd lengths of secrecy which culminated when I questioned A. E. Royce and Harry Bray, the heads of the Ontario Security Commission, and their boss, good old Eric Winkler, in a Legislative committee. I had been fascinated by the government's vague references to a special Ontario criminal investigative body but could never discover anyone who sat on it.

Mr. Shulman:	Have you ever found evidence of hot money being laundered in Ontario?
Mr. Bray:	I cannot answer that.
Mr. Shulman:	What do you mean, you can't answer it?
Mr. Bray:	It is not within my present knowledge. It is not a question I came prepared to answer.

Mr. Shulman:	Mr. Royce?
Mr. Royce:	I don't know.
Mr. Shulman:	Who was responsible – you were represented on this criminal investigation body. Who is your representative on that body?
Mr. Bray:	We are talking about criminal intelligence.
Mr. Shulman:	All right. Whatever it is, who is the representative on the body?
Mr. Bray:	Mr. Minister, I think this is a very difficult field.
Hon. Mr. Winkler:	This is within the purview at the moment of the policy committee, and I wouldn't care to discuss it myself.
Mr. Shulman:	You mean it is a secret who your representative is?
Hon. Mr. Winkler:	Not necessarily, but I am not prepared to discuss it.
Mr. R. Nixon:	Who is it then? Oh come on, Eric, don't get yourself dug into something like that.
Hon. Mr. Winkler:	Well, I don't intend to get myself dug in but I just don't – it's a sensitive area.
Mr. Shulman:	You are not serious. Is it a secret who your representative is on this body?
Hon. Mr. Winkler:	No. Not to me it isn't, of course.
Mr. Shulman:	But it is a secret. You can't tell us?

Hon. Mr. Winkler:	It may not be in the best interests of all concerned.
Mr. Shulman:	Well, why in the world would it be a secret who goes to the meetings?
Mr. Royce:	Security of the state.

Looking back, I suspect that there was no representative, there were no meetings and that the joint criminal investigation body never existed.

In my continuing investigation into organized crime I now blundered into a situation where I compromised myself so seriously that my political career was almost destroyed.

The largest lathing firm in Canada at that time was Acme Lathing. At 1:00 AM on July 1, 1972, the offices of Acme were raked with fire from a machine gun; two weeks later, the building next door to Acme was blown up by a bomb; two nights later, Acme's partner, Gemini Lathing, was also bombed but again the bomb was misplaced and it too accidentally blew up the building next door. The police now put a twenty-four-hour-a-day guard on Acme's premises which they maintained until August 31. On September 1, the guard was cancelled and, on September 2, the entire building was blown up.

On August 30, 1972, a man named Stan Sossin came to my home. Thirtyish, dark, slim and handsome, Sossin introduced himself as one of the owners of Acme Lathing. He then talked for two hours and related a tale of intimidation and violence by union leaders and rival contractors resulting from Acme's refusal to allow organized crime to take over the company and thereby to control the lathing industry.

Acme's troubles had begun in October 1971 when the owners were visited by two men, one the head of the union representing Acme's workers, the other a contractor who owned a small rival lathing firm. Their proposition was very simple. Acme was to merge with the smaller firm and agree to buy all supplies from a third firm which was also in the lathing business. The merged companies would then have effective control of the lathing industry and would immediately raise prices by ten per cent. As the business was then grossing $50 million a year, this would produce an additional profit of $5 million a year, of which one third would go to Acme.

Stan Sossin had flatly refused this offer. The next morning, the union's stewards came onto all of Acme's construction jobs and slowed the work down. When this didn't get Acme to give in, its owners began receiving threatening phone calls. Finally, the machine gunning took place on July 1 and, when Acme still didn't knuckle under, two men were hired to blow up the Acme offices. They were so incompetent that in their first two attempts they blew up neighbouring buildings. They then had to wait until September 1 when they learned from the wife of a police officer that the police guard had been removed. On their third attempt, on September 2, they finally gutted the building.

All of this violence received absolutely no publicity and, as the police seemed unable to take any action, I called in the press and screamed for something to be done. Simultaneously, I phoned Attorney General Al Lawrence and demanded that proper protection be given to Acme, its owners and their families. Lawrence reacted and suddenly there were police everywhere, not only giving protection to Acme but also visiting, following and tapping the phones of the union leaders and the crooked contractors. For three whole days the owners of Acme breathed easier.

Then suddenly ("coincidentally") the three giant insurance companies which Acme used for insuring its buildings and contents sent letters informing Acme that its insurance was being cancelled, adding a little note that the holder of Acme's mortgage was being notified. If the insurance companies had carried out their threat, Acme would have been out of business for its mortgage would automatically have come due and the company would have been forced to the wall. Stan Sossin came to my office completely dejected. "They've beaten us," he said.

I immediately got in touch with the insurance companies. The varying reactions of the three were interesting.

The first company was the most straightforward. After I had explained the situation to their Toronto manager, I concluded, "I find it very interesting that you're co-operating with organized crime." He replied, "Oh no, it isn't that at all – that's just a coincidence. It isn't that we're co-operating with organized crime, it's just that we don't like having losses. We suddenly realized that Acme was too big a risk and, therefore, we're cancelling their insurance. We don't like to carry heavy risks, you know."

I said, "Well, perhaps I misunderstand insurance. Isn't insurance the idea that many thousands of people pool their risks across the country so that the light risks will protect the heavy risks? I can understand your cancelling the insurance on a firm that did something to bring on its own trouble. But here's a firm that's having difficulties only because it stood up against organized crime and you are co-operating with organized crime to put it out of business." The man from the insurance company said, "Well frankly, that is not our business. That's their problem. We're just interested in insurance. And as far as you're concerned, Dr. Shulman, we don't care what you do and we're not going to reinstate that insurance and you can go jump in the lake."

The second company handled me a little more subtly. Their official said, "We'll certainly look into it and phone you back in half an hour." Two days passed and I phoned them again and got the same man on the phone and he said, "Oh yes, yes, what's your number again? Well, we'll phone you back tomorrow for sure." They never did call back.

The third company handled me more cleverly. They said, "Well, that is terrible. That is just a terrible story you've told us Dr. Shulman. We certainly aren't going to do anything that's going to help organized crime and we're going to reinstate the insurance immediately provided the other companies reinstate theirs. After all, you know, we're the smallest one of the bunch as far as insurance goes; why should we take all the risk? But if they're prepared to pool the risk, we'll be glad to go along because we're public spirited and we don't want to do anything that's going to help organized crime."

I was furious and called John Clement, the government minister responsible for the Department of Insurance. I used straight blackmail.

"Look, I don't want to embarrass you with the insurance companies – I know how much they give to the Conservative party – but this is really pretty rough when they take a position that can only help the Mafia. It's going to be awfully embarrassing if I have to get up in the House and say that I came to you as the minister in charge of insurance and you couldn't fix us up."

The minister wasted no time. He ordered the Superintendent of Insurance to call the three companies. Somehow, that day all three changed their minds and decided not to cancel Acme's insurance.

Although the immediate danger was past, obviously Acme and its owners could not receive permanent police protection. In October 1972, I publicly demanded that the government either lay charges against the bombers or order a Royal Commission to look into the violence. I warned that if neither was done I would name in the House the persons who had ordered the bombings.

I was scheduled to give my legislative speech at the beginning of December 1972 and in preparation I routinely approached all my police and undercover contacts. When I phoned detective Max Chikofsky, I struck pay dirt. He told me "Ontario's new Attorney General, Dalton Bales, is involved in this mess. I personally was doing surveillance on the home of Mr. X (one of the contractors accused of being involved in the conspiracy who had previously been convicted of price fixing) and I saw Bales at a party at his home." The Attorney General's Department had been very obviously dragging its feet through this violent summer and I immediately jumped to the conclusion that Bale's connection could be the reason. Chikofsky's information had, up to then, been absolutely correct. But this item was so important and so crucial that I took the precaution of checking with an official from the union for which the detective worked. He confirmed that Chikofsky had reported the same information to him. So did a reporter from the *Globe and Mail* who had been developing a story on the violence for his paper.

And so, I fell for it. On the evening of December 5, 1972, I rose in the House to give my speech on organized crime in the construction industry. I should have realized that something was wrong – almost the entire Tory cabinet was present and it was rare for more than one or two of them to stay in their seats to hear the speech of an opposition member. All went well until I came to the climax of my speech. Hansard records it as follows:

Mr. Shulman: They aren't worried about the police because they know there is not enough evidence to charge them. They weren't worried about the newspapers because they felt that none of this would be printed. They were worried about me giving this speech in the House and producing a Royal Commission; but they weren't too worried about that because they believe they have a powerful friend on the front row of the cabinet. I don't know whether they have or they haven't. They believe they have a powerful friend. However, there is one thing I do know. The police . . .

A GODFATHER BEHIND EVERY BUSH

Mr. Sargent:	Time, time!
Mr. Drea:	We wouldn't want to cut him off.
Mr. Sargent:	He is sick.
Mr. Jessiman:	Right, he's sick!
Mr. Shulman:	From a detective who was assigned for an entirely different reason to watch the home of Mr. X. Just before the last provincial election, the person whom this detective saw to his amazement at this party of X's – it was a fund-raising event for the Conservatives – was Dalton Bales.

All hell now broke loose. Bales jumped to his feet to flatly deny my allegations. He was certainly on solid ground for, in fact, he had *not* been there. Furthermore, he produced a sworn affidavit from Max Chikofsky himself in which Chikofsky (1) stated that he had never seen Bales at this party and (2) had never told me that Bales was there. The uproar in the Legislature was unprecedented – member after member from both the government and the Liberal opposition rose to demand I resign my seat for sullying the reputation of the Attorney General.

Solicitor General John Yaremko began the attack: "The member is irresponsible, completely irresponsible. How many persons have committed suicide lately because of the member for High Park?"

Liberal Vernon Singer got right to the point: "Mr. Speaker, on a point of order, it has always been a custom in democratic legislatures that where a member has charged another member with misconduct and the facts are later found to be incorrect, there is a serious, important and democratic responsibility on the member making the charge that has been proved to be false to resign his seat."

Flamboyant Liberal Eddy Sargent chipped in: "This man can be a character assassin of any of us, of any person in Ontario he wants to libel. He owes the minister an apology and he owes every member of this House an apology. He should do it now."

Premier William Davis gave the final blow: "Honourable members on this side of the House are of the opinion that he owes the House his resignation and is obliged to submit it without condition."

I knew that I had been set up. The affidavit from Chikofsky showed that they had been waiting for me. But it seemed impossible to prove. By now I was so depressed and disgusted that I almost did resign my seat. My waverings were decided by a delegation of reporters from the Provincial Press Gallery who came to me to urge me to fight on. Finally, I offered to resign if the government would call an early by-election. I was certain that my electors would support me but the government would have none of this and in a few days the demands for my resignation were forgotten.

In the excitement and hurly-burly, what was lost was a statement by front bench Conservative member and former Minister of Health Matthew Dymond that he had been at this very party that I had incorrectly alleged Bales had attended. This produced no comment from anyone. I found it a little hard to accept that it was such a sin to have falsely accused a minister of such an association – while the fact of another minister having exactly the same association was ignored.

My suspicions that the government had been waiting for me were confirmed months later when Tory backbencher Charlie McIlveen wrote in a newsletter to his constituents: "When he opened his speech I thought something was up because all members of the justice policy field were in attendance. There were the Hon. George Kerr, the Provincial Secretary for Justice; the Hon. Dalton Bales, the Attorney General; the Hon.

John Yaremko, the Solicitor General; the Hon. Syl
Apps, Minister of Correctional Services. This alone is
unusual. But with ten other cabinet ministers also in
attendance, it indicated they thought Morty had an
unusual speech prepared."

In the aftermath of my humiliation, the facts I had
released before my blunder began to be re-examined by
the press and editorial questions were asked.

Harold Greer wrote a column printed in many Ontario
papers saying:

> If the government really believes he should resign, the
> proper course is to refer his conduct to the Legislature's
> committee on privileges and elections with a view to
> securing at least a motion of censure. Even then, Dr.
> Shulman would not be obliged to resign, although the
> Legislature could bar him from taking his seat.

> The government has not pursued such a course and Mr.
> Davis, pressed by reporters to explain why, repeatedly
> refused to comment. The explanation is obvious enough:
> the government is afraid of Dr. Shulman and what an
> inquiry might reveal.

> Dr. Shulman, for example, still insists Max Chikofsky
> told him Mr. Bales was at —'s fund-raising party. Mr.
> Bales has tacitly admitted there is a police intelligence
> report which contains the same information and identi-
> fied Chikofsky as the source. The *Globe and Mail* has
> said Chikofsky told one of its reporters the same thing in
> an unpublished interview last October 6. Fred Leger,
> business representative of the Carpenters' Union, has said
> that Chikofsky told him that Bales was there.

> At the very least an inquiry into Dr. Shulman's speech
> would have to establish why, if four people say Mr.
> Chikofsky told them he saw Mr. Bales, he now says he
> didn't. The answer to that could well prove the need for
> a Royal Commission into organized crime in the con-
> struction industry, something the government has been
> rejecting for over a year.

Premier Davis was not very happy with the situation and he solved his embarrassment by ordering that a Royal Commission be set up to investigate the role of organized crime in the construction industry.

The new investigation was not welcomed by the construction industry. Alex Main, manager of the Toronto Building Trades Council, denounced it as "a stupid witch hunt." He went on, "I don't know of any reasons that we need a Royal Commission but at least it will clear the air by forcing Shulman to put up or shut up."

The men attached to the Commission took their assignment seriously and instituted a detailed investigation of the whole mess. On December 18, 1974, Commissioner Judge Waisberg brought in his report. It concluded: "Considering all of this evidence it is a reasonable inference that there existed at that time an association of persons for the purpose of conducting illegal activities. I am of the opinion that the measures taken succeeded in blocking these activities in the sectors of the construction industry under investigation. I suspect that it has been made clear to all, that activities in the construction industry are subject to the same rules of law that govern the community at large."

The report found that there was indeed a Mafia organization in Ontario with its own godfather, that one of Metro's largest builders had links to organized crime and that six union leaders were unfit for their jobs. It made detailed recommendations to prevent recurrence of the graft and the violence.

The Royal Commission did its job well. The glare of publicity was anathema to the criminals and by the end of 1974 they had completely abandoned this aspect of their activities and tranquillity had returned to the construction industry. I was pleased about these results. But the Bales-Chikofsky memory continued to rankle me. I tried to force Chikofsky to tell the truth by laying charges against him at the private investigators' licensing board run by the OPP, on the technical grounds that he had improperly given me privileged information. I might just as well not have bothered: at the hearing, Chikofsky did not take the stand and his licence was not cancelled. The board merely reprimanded him and that was that. I guess I'll never know the "why" of that story.

One very unfortunate aftermath of my speech took place almost immediately when twenty-five police chiefs belonging to the Criminal Intelligence Service of Ontario voted "no confidence" in the Ontario Police Commission because they claimed that someone there was leaking confidential reports to me. What caused this upset was a Keystone Cops investigation carried out by the OPP following a decision by the Ontario government to establish off-track betting shops. In preparation for this, the OPP had been asked to investigate the two firms manufacturing the required equipment to be sure that neither was involved with organized crime. The form the "investigation" took was for the OPP intelligence officers to visit the president of each firm and ask if the firm was associated with the Mafia. Both gentlemen, of course, gave the proper assurances. Unfortunately for the OPP, these naïve intelligence reports fell into my hands and I read them into the Legislative record.

My source for the reports was the same mysterious "deep throat" in the Attorney General's department who had been sending me information right along. But the government decided that my source was one Inspector Herbert Thurston of the Ontario Police Commission whom they promptly fired. I have never met or spoken to Thurston, either before or since that time. And I made haste to rise in the Legislature to assure Solicitor General John Yaremko that Thurston was innocent. But he wouldn't listen to me. Thurston stayed fired!

38 *Mimico*

Barely had the Bales furor died down when I got involved in a battle with Syl Apps, a minister with whom I usually had excellent rapport. Over the previous six months I had received an ever-increasing flood of letters from inmates of various penal institutions asking my assistance in getting them transferred to the Alex G. Brown Memorial Clinic, an institution to which the provincial penal authorities commonly referred prisoners for treatment for drug addiction. Convicts were normally transferred there close to the end of their sentence and stayed a maximum of six months.

The Alex G. Brown had never before been a popular place and I couldn't understand its sudden upsurge in attractiveness. The mystery was solved when a prisoner at Guelph who had been directed to be transferred to the Alex G. Brown begged Dr. G. Nagy, the visiting vice-chairman of the Ontario Parole Board, *not* to have him transferred because, as he put it, "I am trying to get off drugs and this is impossible at Alex G. Brown because drugs are so freely available there." Nagy was astounded and forwarded this allegation up the chain of command to the Minister of Correctional Services, Syl Apps, who ordered a secret investigation.

The investigation was carried out by the inspection

branch of the Department of Correctional Services. To the dismay of the institution's senior staff, the inspectors found that not only were drugs and alcohol freely available to the inmates of the Alex G. Brown but that part of that supply was being made available by a staff member who was selling to the inmates.

The inspectors discovered that the major reason why this prison had turned into a drug addict's heaven was that prisoners were not searched before or after visits from friends or relatives nor after temporary weekend absences. When the inspector questioned Mr. N. Cramp, the Chief Supervisor, he found him to be very much against the searching of the inmates "because it is against all clinic policies and would break down the trust and honour between staff and inmates."

I visited the Alex G. Brown and interviewed superintendent E.K. Glinfort. The superintendent said he was aware of the rumour "around town" about drugs in the institution but said that the rumour was "grossly exaggerated." Any convicts caught using drugs were shipped out to other institutions as soon as they were caught. He also told me that eight out of the current sixty-six were shipped out the previous week!

Mr. Glinfort said that there was better control of drugs in his institution than in any other jail because of the taking of spot urine tests. He admitted that a staff member had "resigned" the week before but, when I asked if this was because he was selling drugs to the inmates, he replied, "I think that you will understand that I cannot confirm or deny that."

Three days later I received anonymously in the mail a copy of the confidential report made by the inspection department. Inspector D. Webb concluded his damning seven-page indictment of the Alex G. Brown by saying:

> At this point there is sufficient evidence to support the allegation of inmate M. made to Dr. Nagy in the interview

of 17 August, 1972, contained in Dr. Nagy's letter to Mr. F.H. Potts dated 18 August, 1972. There is sufficient evidence to support his statement to me at Guelph C.C. . . .

There is a rumour of junior staff discontent at not being supported from the disciplinary point of view, and of being faulted because they sabotage the programmes by exerting any discipline. Also being told so in front of the inmate.

The higher echelon at the Clinic is obviously a very close-knit group and resent any questioning of their policies. By reason of this it was not advisable to interview any junior staff, who fear repercussions.

It is very obvious that the patients generally are not as trustworthy as the Administration like to believe.

Any further investigation may prejudice the Clinic's programmes in that junior staff who give statements must be protected, procedures must be questioned and explained, and statements will have to be taken from both senior and professional staff.

What upset me mightily was that, although Webb's report had been made six weeks earlier, the ministry had taken no action. I promptly released the report to the press and the minister only then promised to tighten up security. It wasn't Syl Apps' finest hour. But it was one of his few bad times. Syl Apps was a good minister, one of Canada's greatest sportsmen and perhaps the finest gentleman ever to grace the government benches.

39 *The Happy Hooker*

Things were fairly quiet for me in the Legislature for the next few months but, at the end of March 1973, I became involved in a bizarre and amusing controversy over Xaviera Hollander, the famous former prostitute. Miss Hollander's raunchy book, *The Happy Hooker*, had been on the stands for over a year and had sold over seventeen million copies world-wide when the Toronto police morality squad suddenly became aware of it and ordered the distributor, Metro Toronto News, to remove the book from sale or face criminal charges. Metro News didn't even fight. The books came out of the stores and I became very concerned – not about Xaviera Hollander, who is quite capable of looking after herself, but about the whole idea of the police deciding what we are allowed to read. Since the booksellers were afraid to fight back, I decided to do so for them and on March 29 I opened a book store in my office at Queen's Park selling *The Happy Hooker* at $1.50 with ten per cent off to MPPs. I notified the morality squad that the books were on sale and dared them to charge me so that the courts could settle the censorship issue.

Business was brisk and I quickly sold 250 books but the morality squad didn't show up to make the arrest. Instead, they meekly backed down and, when they failed to charge me, the dealers began to restock *The Happy Hooker.*

For once, I received universal press acclaim. But my mail showed me that Archie Bunker was still very much alive and well in Ontario. Here is a sample of the three hundred-odd letters that poured in:

"You are out of your mind and should be ashamed of yourself."

"Pornography and smut are the worst forms of pollution going down in society today. How you can say that freedom is the availability of such cultural gems as the memoirs of a prostitute is totally beyond me."

"I'd much prefer to have Metro Police on my side than that immoral whore who was thrown out of the States. If Metro Police can't say what's good for us who can?"

"I have not read the book but I watched the whore on television and she said she was heterosexual (*sic*) and would have intercourse with man or woman. She said she liked sex and could stand lots of it and she liked lots of variety."

"I think that by your action you have not only lost a lot of support, particularly from women, but you have made your own personal contribution to the decadence of our society. Alas, my idol had feet of clay!"

"You are getting nuttier every day and we will have to do something about it. You should be locked up in a mental institution and not allowed to run loose at all."

"You are a dirty old man."

"We are in this world, Sir, to lift people higher; not to help keep their minds in a filthy sewer or dungeon. When you are willing to allow this putrid muck on the book stalls for people to buy, you are helping to thrust them down, push them under, as surely as if you had engaged in the physical act of violence."

"You must know how much wrong action comes from reading filth in the first place. People are in prison today

for offences which are directly attributable to their reading indecent books or viewing indecent pictures in the
first place."

The final word came from Xaviera herself. The lady
phoned and cooed, "Now that you have done me such a
big favour, let me do something for you." She followed
this up with a number of suggestions that surprised even
me. Alas, they are unprintable, except perhaps in one of
her books. Regretfully I declined, explaining, "Politicians
are not allowed to accept bribes, even after the fact!"

40 *Ripping Off the Door*

Just three weeks after getting all that abuse over *The Happy Hooker*, I ran into flack from another direction. It came about because, after my last voting fiasco with Russell Rowe, I had once again stopped going through the motions and walked out whenever a vote was called. Unfortunately for me, when the vote on the second reading of the raise in the new Sales Tax was taken, every other member did vote and the *Globe and Mail* wrote a front page story pointing out that I was the only opposition member who did not show his displeasure by casting a vote against this unpopular tax. Stephen Lewis was not happy and made a point of asking me to be sure to be present at the third and final vote on the bill which was due to take place on the evening of May 14th.

I thought I had better be there early and so I sat through two hours of repetitious and boring speeches and finally told NDP whip Jack Stokes that I was going back to my office to work and would return in thirty minutes.

It is the custom at Queen's Park to summon the members to their seats when a vote is called by the ringing of a bell. When the bell stops ringing, the clerks of the House lock the doors so that no one can enter or leave. Some thirty-five minutes later I returned to the Chamber. But just as I was about to enter the door, the bells announcing the vote stopped ringing.

I tried the door and found that it had just been locked. With horrible visions of another front page embarrassment, I gave the door a mighty wrench in an attempt to attract the clerk's attention – but unfortunately thereby ripping the door from its hinges!

I was startled but not too startled to take advantage of the suddenly gaping door. I ran inside to take my seat. But to my dismay, a tremendous uproar arose from the Conservative backbenchers who insisted that I be thrown out. My fellow opposition members urged me to hold my seat. The Sergeant-at-Arms was already reaching for his ceremonial sword.

Fortunately, the cool head of Speaker Alan Reuter prevailed. He ruled that I could remain in the Chamber but that my vote would not be counted. In the ensuing uproar, the Conservatives bellowed their demands that I be thrown out while I insisted that the government was saving themselves from my vote on a technicality.

What everyone seemed to overlook was that the government had over a twenty-vote majority in the House anyway – so that whether or not I voted was really quite irrelevant.

But it wasn't just the Tory MPPs who were angry with me. My fellow NDPs were not happy with either my battles or the publicity they received and I now found myself under attack from my own party. It started when the Quebec government cancelled their tax on the sale of stocks and, as a result, huge stock orders began to be transferred from the Toronto Stock Exchange to Montreal. In order to help prevent Toronto's stock brokers from going bankrupt, I appealed to the government who responded responsibly by cancelling Ontario's security tax. This produced an immediate attack by NDP frontbenchers Mike Cassidy and Pat Lawlor while I now found myself in the embarrassing position of hearing

Treasurer John White defend the government's actions by quoting my speeches!

Barely had this died down when the question of local option (whether or not liquor sales should be permitted in the area) came up and, although I do enjoy my wine, I defended High Park's right to majority rule, that is, to remain dry if they so wished. This resulted in a bitter attack on me by left-wing NDP member Bud Germa who demanded that the undemocratic practice of the majority in an area deciding on their liquor amenities be abolished.

Fortunately there were pleasant moments amid these aggravations. The Miss Nude Canada contest asked me to judge who was the prettiest of their contestants and I accepted the duty with alacrity. I never did get to the contest, however, for my wife "persuaded" me that it was a terrible thing to do politically and anyway, "Don't you see enough naked women in your office?" I couldn't convince her that it wasn't the same and reluctantly withdrew from the judging.

41 *Wire Tapping Again*

John Yaremko had now become the Solicitor General. He was an easy mark because of his determination not to anger his ethnic supporters from downtown Toronto's Bellwoods riding. This led him to make the headline-producing statement in the House that there was a certain five-letter word one should not use because it was slanderous toward Italians – MAFIA. Yaremko never did recover from this gaffe and I found it easy to goad him into making a fool of himself.

On May 23, 1973, I set Yaremko up by asking him in the Legislature if the OPP had tapped the telephone of any NDP candidate or their publicity director during the 1971 election. He answered, "No, there were no telephone taps of this nature to my knowledge." I knew that either Yaremko's answer was untrue or else that he didn't know what his own police were up to. I made haste to play a tape that I had in my possession.

This tape had been left lying on my desk that morning along with an accompanying note saying that the tape had come from OPP files and that it had been accidentally lost by a police officer who had had too much to drink. On the tape were recordings of conversations between the defeated NDP candidate in Prescott riding, one Yvon Montpetit, and his publicity director, arms dealer John

St. Amour. I suspect that it was St. Amour rather than Montpetit who was being tapped. But the most embarrassing aspect of the affair for the police was that the tape also contained a conversation between Chief Superintendent Al Duguid of the OPP and an RCMP intelligence officer discussing security plans in connection with Quebec's FLQ. The police were horribly embarrassed at being caught taping each other's conversations while Yaremko was furious at the police for losing their tapes and at me for revealing it. We ended up roaring at each other in the Legislature. It began very quietly:

Mr. Shulman:	I would like to ask the minister, when I get his attention . . .
Hon. Mr. Yaremko:	The honourable member has my attention. I don't have to look at him to have my attention.
Mr. Shulman:	Oh, I thank you very much; that is very kind.
Hon. Mr. Yaremko:	I can be looking the other way and still be paying attention.
Mr. Shulman:	Mr. Chairman, why do the OPP senior officers tape their conversations with the RCMP?
Hon. Mr. Yaremko:	Mr. Chairman, it is just a matter of keeping notes, of keeping a record of what has transpired. The RCMP would be aware that the note-taking by taping was taking place.
Mr. Shulman:	I would like to ask the minister is there not a law in this country that if one is going to tape a conversation he must not only inform the other person but have a beeper on the phone? Is there no requirement that one must notify a person if he is going to tape their conversations?

Hon. Mr. Yaremko:	Mr. Chairman, in practice the RCMP would be aware that this note-taking via taping was taking place.
Mr. Shulman:	They wouldn't tell them at the beginning of each specific conversation? They know that all the conversations are being taped, do they?
Hon. Mr. Yaremko:	I would assume that the general practice would be known to the parties involved.
Mr. Shulman:	After these conversations with the RCMP, what does the OPP do with the tapes?
Hon. Mr. Yaremko:	I am sorry, Mr. Chairman, my attention was diverted for a moment. Would the honourable member repeat the question?
Mr. Shulman:	Oh, I thought I always had your attention, even when your head was turned away. I'm sorry.
Hon. Mr. Yaremko:	My head wasn't turned away, unfortunately.
Mr. Shulman:	You were looking at me and I thought I had your attention. Mr. Chairman, what do the OPP do with these tapes that they make of their conversations with the RCMP after they have finished making them?
Hon. Mr. Yaremko:	Well, they are shared with other members of the force who would be involved in the matter being looked at.
Mr. Shulman:	Are they kept under some security or are they just sort of put on a shelf in the public part of the OPP offices?

Hon. Mr. Yaremko: Yes, high security.

Mr. Shulman: High security. Can the minister explain how the OPP managed to lose their tapes?

Hon. Mr. Yaremko: Which tape is the honourable member referring to?

Mr. Shulman: Well, I'll play you one.

Mr. Chairman: No. Order, please. It's improper to play a tape recorder in here – just the same as it is to tape or record or . . .

Mr. Shulman: I cannot play the tape, but I'll try and describe it to the minister, if I may. It is a tape made at the beginning of October, 1971. It was a phone call made by your Chief Inspector, a Mr. Al Duguid, to the Intelligence Branch at the RCMP in which he is discussing with them his worries about a possible uprising or trouble at the time of the anniversary of the FLQ disturbance the previous year. He expresses certain dates when this might occur, October 5 or 6 or 16, 1971. At the beginning of the tape, before the RCMP officer comes on, he says, "I've got mine going," referring to the taping. That's the tape I'm referring to. I am asking how could it be that your officer, your Chief Superintendent, would manage to lose that tape?

Hon. Mr. Yaremko: Mr. Chairman, first of all, the honourable member is asking the question "how did the Chief Inspector happen to lose it?" He is making a statement of fact. There is no evi-

	dence that it was lost by that officer. Of course, I think one of the important questions, Mr. Chairman, is how did that tape come into the hands of the honourable member for High Park?
Mr. Shulman:	Exactly!
Hon. Mr. Yaremko:	We are getting a full investigation under way. I think that this is no laughing matter, the way the honourable member has on his face. This is one of the most serious things that can happen, when an item of high security, which evidently related to the investigation of criminal activity – finds itself in the hands of the honourable member either directly or, I assume, indirectly. I think this is a matter which is of importance not only to this Legislature but to the people of the Province of Ontario – and I have no knowledge of the details – that when a piece of material comes into the hands of somebody, he should take it upon himself, indiscriminately, to utilize it for political advantage.

The exchange quickly degenerated ending with the minister and me trading insults. There never was any explanation forthcoming and, like so many other matters, this one was just forgotten. If Yaremko's investigation ever did discover what had happened, he certainly didn't tell me.

42 *The Maid of the Mist*

On July 15, 1973, I received an anonymous phone call: "Do you want to see a heroin shipment go into the U.S.A.? Will you pay me for the information? Will you promise not to turn me in? Drive to Niagara Falls tomorrow and register at the Brock Sheraton. I'll contact you there."

I drove to Niagara Falls as instructed and took a room overlooking the falls. Just after noon, my room phone rang and the same voice instructed me to go downstairs to the front door where I would be picked up by a car. Sure enough, as I walked out the door a taxi was waiting for me. I climbed in to find a very ordinary looking man sitting in the back seat. He was about thirty-five, well dressed, average appearance – not my image of a heroin smuggler. He motioned me to silence and we sat quietly until the taxi drove us across the Peace Bridge. U.S. Customs passed us uneventfully and we left the taxi at the edge of the park. I was bitterly disappointed.

"Don't tell me that's it. I suppose you're going to say you had the drugs in your pocket!"

He laughed. "Oh no. I'm not crazy. I would not carry any drugs across like that. What if they had searched me? No, the shit is still back on the Canadian side."

He now led me into the park to the U.S. entrance to the *Maid of the Mist* boat ride under the falls. We rode down the elevator and purchased two tickets. But, we did not join the line of people waiting to board the boat. Instead, my guide led me back to the elevator and, up top again, he hailed a taxi to take us back to Canada.

On the Canadian side, he dropped me from the cab and instructed me to buy two tickets to board the *Maid of the Mist* and told me he would join me before I boarded. Sure enough, he appeared beside me fifteen minutes later. We were given oil slickers for the spray and walked aboard along with some forty tourists. As we boarded, an attendant punched our tickets and told us to keep them as they would have to be surrendered when we debarked. I noticed my companion drop them over the side. Ten minutes later, we emerged from the spray and wind under Niagara Falls and the boat docked on the American side. The mate called out, "American ticket holders only debark here." But we got off, surrendering the two American tickets purchased earlier, now neatly punched by my companion's puncher.

As we once again ascended to the park, he opened his coat and showed me a thick money belt. "That's it and goodbye."

"Wait. One question," I pleaded. "Why have you shown me this?"

"Hell," he replied, "I don't like it any better than you. I had to make these trips but this is my last one. Once I'm clear you can tell the cops. I'd like it stopped." He walked away.

As soon as I returned to Toronto, I phoned the general manager of the company running the *Maid of the Mist* boats, a Mr. Don Wilson. I explained the situation and asked him to change their schedule so that boats leaving from the Canadian side return to the same side and similarly on the U.S. side. He refused, saying that it was more efficient making a round trip. "We do with three boats what would take five if we were to make that change." As for the smuggling, he suggested that I contact the RCMP. I wrote them the same day but they were not impressed. On September 7, 1973, they wrote to me, "Our investigation has not disclosed any evidence that smuggling of persons or contraband is occurring on the *Maid of the Mist* vessels. I do agree, however, that this method of smuggling could be used because the *Maid of the Mist* vessels do stop at both sides of the Niagara River."

I guess that the heroin is still going across the same way.

43 *Chiropractors*

In politics one can freely criticize Liberals, Conservatives, New Democrats, doctors, dentists, lawyers, the U.S.A. or the U.S.S.R. But, if one wishes to be re-elected, there are certain *verboten* subjects which bear no criticism. These include the Queen, Israel, blacks, religion, strikers, scientology and, above all, chiropractors.

As a doctor, I had always had vague suspicions about chiropractors. But as an elected politician, I made a point of avoiding the subject until, in 1973, I learned of a case so terrible that my conscience would not let it go by.

At the beginning of 1973, a doctor came to me because an eleven-year-old patient of his with cystic fibrosis had discontinued treatment. The child's mother had believed a story told to her by a chiropractor that the boy's trouble was "subluxation of the second vertical vertebrae" and that, with chiropractic treatments, the boy could be cured within twelve months. I was appalled at this story because it is absolutely certain that cystic fibrosis *cannot* be cured by manipulation of the spine. I sent a complaint to the Board of Chiropractic. They wrote me back saying that, in their opinion, the chiropractor was doing nothing wrong.

My dismay was compounded when I found that the

President of the Ontario Chiropractic Association was distributing literature which stated that spinal misalignments caused "headaches, high blood pressure, eye troubles, tonsillitis, whooping cough, asthma, pleurisy, pneumonia, jaundice, diabetes, ulcers, anaemia, nephritis, acne, boils, diarrhea, hernias, appendicitis and haemorrhoids."

Even worse, the Dean of the Canadian Memorial Chiropractic College had written a textbook recommending chiropractic in the treatment of "peptic ulcers, some malignancies and emphysema."

I had got nowhere in my correspondence with the chiropractors. And so, in October 1973, I made a speech in the Legislature. In preparing this speech, I had been able to use material leaked to me by Ontario's new Minister of Health, Richard Potter, who wanted someone to tackle the chiropractors in order to give him an excuse to act. I used Potter's material from OHIP to show that chiropractors were billing the government to treat "acne, arthritis, bed wetting, constipation, eye strain, varicose veins, hay fever" and a dozen other complaints in the treatment of which they had no competence. Moreover, some chiropractors were routinely X-raying unnecessarily the spines of apparently healthy children – producing God knows how much leukemia and cancer twenty years later in their lives. I urged the government to crack down on the quacks in chiropractic.

In response:

(1) The Executive Director of the Ontario Chiropractic Association accused me of "sensationalism, gross ignorance, false statements, false implications, etc."

(2) The Board of Directors of Chiropractic ordered their members not to hand out any more of the literature I had criticized.

(3) Otherwise, nothing really changed – no chiropractors lost their licence nor were any sent back to school for re-education.

No other MPP took up this war. Politically it was just too dangerous and I certainly failed in my battle. There is still a textbook in the library of the Canadian Memorial Chiropractic College written by the ex-Dean, advising manipulation of the back in patients who have just suffered heart attacks.

Where chiropractics are concerned, I have decided that there is no limit to the stupidity of the public or the spinelessness (no pun intended) of their representatives.

44 *I Join the CIA*

In January 1974, I made another of my speeches about organized crime, in this case describing how the Mafia used Ontario for "washing" or legalizing its hot funds. I gave a number of examples, pointing out that the OPP could do nothing about it because there was no law in Canada making this kind of manoeuvre an offence. The day after I gave the speech, two young OPP intelligence officers came to my office, introduced themselves and said, "We're both after the same enemy so why don't we work together? Instead of attacking us in the Legislature, let's discuss these cases together and do our best to fight these criminals."

Of course I didn't hesitate and, as a result, began a close relationship with the dedicated officers in the OPP intelligence squad. I made my files available to them and they, in turn, were most co-operative in helping me research out my problem cases. The association went beautifully and, on April 10, 1974, I was invited by Ontario Police Intelligence to go with two of their officers on one of their periodic liaison visits to Michigan in connection with organized crime. I jumped at the chance and the three of us drove to Detroit on June 4. We spent the next three days in Detroit, Southfield and Lansing, meeting members of various police forces, municipal, state and federal, plus a number of detectives from private agencies. I was told of their problems and given suggestions as how best to combat organized crime in Canada. They showed me their equipment and advised me of the latest wrinkles in Mafia-type crimes. I returned to Canada on June 7 with a briefcase filled with model legislation and a head spinning with stories and ideas.

Unfortunately, on my return, I made the foolish mistake of telling an old reporter "friend," one Gerald McAulife, about my trip. His newspaper blood proved stronger than friendship and he told the story to his editor at Toronto's *Globe and Mail*. It seemed incredible to the *Globe* that an opposition politician would be included in an official police trip and so they concluded that some nefarious deal had been concocted between the police and myself. The next day's newspaper had a front page article headlined, "Shulman Denies Making Deal with Government to raise Mafia Questions in Legislature." The article consisted of expressions of surprise at my trip, plus accusations that I had somehow returned with confidential government documents. The latter accusation was quite untrue and, as the *Globe* was unable to find a shred of corroborating evidence, they quickly dropped the matter. I thought it was forgotten by everyone.

Not quite everyone, however. The National Caucus of Labour is a left-wing splinter group on the fringes of the labour movement in the north-east U.S.A. who then had as their central belief an irrational fear that Nelson Rockefeller was plotting to take over the world. (Today they think it is David Rockefeller.) Every event from the downfall of Nixon to the Arab-Israeli war was viewed by them as part of Rockefeller's overall plot and his selection as Vice-President by Gerald Ford threw them into a paroxysm of hysteria. Prior to 1974, I had never heard of them nor, I suspect, they of me. But a coincidence would convince them that I was the CIA operative in charge of Rockefeller's interests in Canada and the northern U.S.A.!

Beginning in the forties, the FBI had heavily infiltrated the U.S. Communist party with undercover agents until, by the late fifties, in cities like Chicago almost one quarter of the membership were FBI operatives. Some of these men and women have been working within the Communist party for so long that they have risen to national leadership of that organization.

This type of infiltration was very easy for the FBI for the simple reason that, beginning in 1946, there were so very few legitimate new recruits that the Communists grabbed any prospective new member. The FBI agents were hard working, industrious, and anxious to participate so it was easy for them to rise in the party.

The rise of Maoism in the sixties posed an entirely new problem. Suddenly, numerous little groups containing only a few members began popping up all over the country, each with their own strange brand of left-wing philosophy. There were some who followed the teachings of Mao, some those of Trotsky, and even some who called themselves true Marxist-Leninist Communists in contrast to the old line Communist party with its loyalty to Moscow. The difficulties for the FBI in infiltrating these tiny groups were immense. And yet it was far more important to be aware of their activities because of their penchant for violence and irrational activities. Following the Patricia Hearst debacle in the spring of 1974, instructions went out to all FBI regional officers to vastly increase their activities among these fringe left-wing groups.

In early 1974, the Detroit unit of the FBI succeeded in infiltrating one of its agents, Vernon Higgins, into the National Caucus of Labour Committee membership in Pontiac, Michigan. All went well for some months but, on June 6, the other members of the committee became suspicious of Higgins, grabbed him, scared the hell out

190 Member of the Legislature

of him and made him confess to being an FBI agent. The police were quickly alerted and, within hours, thirteen armed Detroit police and FBI agents raided the Labour Committee offices, laid charges over the kidnapping of Higgins and seized all the files in the office. Actually, this was the prime purpose of the whole operation – with the files, the FBI now had the entire membership list.

At the time I knew nothing of all this but I became involved because of the article in the *Globe and Mail.* The members of the Labour Caucus found the coincidence of the raid on their headquarters and my visit to Detroit no coincidence. Beginning the week after the *Globe* story, their New York paper, *New Solidarity*, began a series of articles on my sins as Rockefeller's representative and the cause of all their troubles. They were not prepared to be convinced of reality. And they accompanied their newspaper tirades with a liberal sprinkling of nasty phone calls and letters.

Here's their write up of June 26, 1974:

> Ontario June 23. The fast-breaking series of events this week - just three weeks before the critical Canadian national elections – makes clear Rockefeller's determination to subvert the elections by harassing and disrupting the campaign of the only opposition to his plans for a military takeover of Canada – the North American Labour Party (NALP).

> On June 29, a story broke on the front page of the Toronto *Globe and Mail* "leaking" an unprecedented three-day trip to Michigan by a leading member of the CIA-created New Democratic Party (NDP), Morton Shulman, MP, from the High Park District of Toronto. Shulman went to Michigan accompanied by two Ontario provincial police intelligence agents to meet with police intelligence units in Detroit and Lansing. That same day thirteen agents of the CIA, FBI and the Detroit police illegally entered the Detroit Labour Committee office, guns drawn, and stole the names and addresses of key Canadian contacts . . .

Initial intelligence on Shulman's background links him intimately to the CIA-controlled counter-insurgency network in Canada. Aside from his membership in the CIA's own Canadian countergang, the NDP, Shulman was assigned to the Michigan trip by Liberal Party Solicitor General Kerr who is firmly connected to the search-and-seal operations recently carried out in Quebec and the Great Lakes Horseshoe area . . .

Shulman was indicted for crimes against humanity under the Nuremberg statutes last year by the Labour Committee for his book, *How to Make Millions*, a recounting of his gory killings on the Canadian commodity markets where capitalists profit from the destruction of the living standard of the working class.

The key to Shulman's presence in Michigan is revealed by an article he authored just last week for his regular column in the Toronto *Sun*, comparing Canada now to Uruguay fifteen years ago. At that time, Uruguay was hit by runaway inflation and, according to Shulman, as a result there sprang up "young ideologues" called the Tupamaros who went around kidnapping CIA agents. Shulman notes that Canada today is in the same situation and must beware of the same type of terrorist kidnappings by similar groups . . .

An interview with the managing editor of the *Globe and Mail*, the newspaper which broke the story of Shulman's trip, confirmed that the "Mafia" connection is a cover for Shulman's real purpose. Asked about the trip's function he replied, "Yes, well . . . we have a lot more information than we printed concerning the trip . . . we know a thing or two . . ." Asked directly if Shulman is a CIA agent he paused, then said, "I don't think so."

At first I was amused. But the nuts from the American Labour Party became a terrible nuisance. They came to all of my speeches and set up a terrible chant, "Down with the CIA! Down with Shulman – the CIA's agent!" Finally, at a speech at McMaster University, one young and attractive but demented girl made so much noise that I couldn't be heard. Finally I asked her, "What do

I have to do to quiet you?" She responded, "Admit you're a CIA agent." I quickly said, "Yes, I admit it," and she let me finish my speech.

The next week's issue of *New Solidarity* was headlined "CIA agent confesses his role!" They continued to denounce me regularly even after I quit politics.

45 *I Bomb the SEC*

Some of the controversies I became involved in were a little less than earthshaking. Here is an extract from Hansard that spring:

Mr. Shulman: Mr. Speaker, I have a number of serious matters that I would like to discuss in this Throne debate but before I come to them, may I just take a very few moments for one that is not quite so serious. I think perhaps I have involved our province in a war and I thought I should let the members know about it. Before I begin, I think we all must have solidarity in here. We have our differences but when one of our members is in trouble, I think we must all stick together to help him out because the one who is in trouble is me.

The situation is that some eight years ago I wrote a book which caused some surprise to the publisher and myself in that it sold remarkably well. There is an organization in Washington called the Securities and Exchange Commission. Two months ago they discovered I had written this book and they sent me a very official letter in which they say that they have just discovered my activities. Although normally they do not insist on taking into their fold foreigners who write a single book on the market, to quote them, they say, "Your activities seem to clearly involve you in being in the business of advising others for compensation through publications as to the advisability of investing in securities." The letter finishes off, "Would you please inform us in writing of your intentions with regard to registration." It's signed Allan Rosenblat, chief counsel of the Securities and Exchange Commission, Washington, D.C.

Hon. J. T. Clement*: It's about time they caught up with the member.

Hon. A. Grossman†: The member gets the message.

Mr. Shulman: Right, that's the way I felt about it. Well, I was terribly flattered. I mean if the U.S. government thinks I am an investment adviser, I thought that would be very nice and that I would put that after my name – Morton Shulman, MD, MPP, IA, for investment adviser. So I wrote them back and I said, "Thanks very much, that's really great."

One thing that puzzled me: I received the letter on February 26, 1974 and it was dated January 3, 1973. I couldn't figure out whether the mails had really slowed down

*Minister of Consumer and Commercial Relations
†Provincial Secretary for Resources Development

there or whether they were confused which year it was but, finally, I figured out they didn't know which year it was. The other thing that bothered me was that it was addressed to Dr. Morton Shulman, care of the Book of the Month Club, Camp Hill, Pennsylvania. That may have had something to do with the delay in getting to me.

But, anyway, I wrote them back and said, "Gee, thanks fellows, that's great. If you think I'm an investment adviser, I'd be delighted to register and have those initials after my name. Send me the forms."

That was all very well until the forms arrived. There was a twenty-five page form to fill out and the first question was, "What are your qualifications as an investment adviser?" Well, I really have no formal qualifications so I wrote down "none." That's right, Mr. Speaker, you have to tell the truth when you are dealing with a government agency.

I filled out this twenty-five page form and then I thought, before I send this down to the American Government, maybe I should have some lawyer see it. He said, "Gee Morty, you had better not send it down because as soon as they see your first answer, 'none,' they are going to refuse your registration as an investment adviser and then you will be a failed investment adviser and, as a failed investment adviser, they'll be able to get the U.S. courts to stop you selling books in the States and that would be bad."

Interjections by honourable members.

Mr. Shulman: I wrote back to them and said, "Look, under these regulations it says I don't have to register if I have less than fifteen clients. I only really give advice to one person. That's my wife and she doesn't follow it anyway so I don't think that counts. The second thing is that you are exempt if you have less than fifteen clients and you do not generally hold yourself out as an investment adviser. I really don't hold myself out as an investment adviser. I generally hold myself out as a statesman. Would you advise me what I should do?"

That all seemed very well until on my birthday they sent me this letter and I thought it was in very bad form really. Anyway, it was dated April 2, 1974 and it's from the Securities and Exchange Commission, Washington, D.C. It is no longer addressed "Dear Dr. Shulman;" it's addressed "Dear Mr. Shulman."

Hon. Mr. Grossman: They took a couple of initials away.

Mr. Shulman: It starts off: "Compliance with the federal securities law is no laughing matter." They then proceed to lay out the various horrendous penalties that can happen to me if I don't cooperate with them. Apparently, huge fines are possible and – what else? – twenty years in jail for each book that's sold.

Hon. Mr. Grossman: The next thing is they'll take the member away and give him a number.

Mr. Shulman:	Well, I felt that this was a hostile act, Mr. Speaker. I wrote back to the securities commission in the United States and I said, "I feel that you're carrying out a hostile act. I'm not quite sure how you are going to carry out all these things, short of sending in the Marines. I know what American strategy is and . . .
Hon. Mr. Grossman:	We don't have Marines.
Mr. Shulman:	. . . unfortunately, my province has very little military capability." But I've been in touch with the Minister of Natural Resources (Mr. Bernier) and he has some forty-five planes he uses for fighting fires. I have requested him to do a pre-emptive water bombing strike on the SEC building in Washington. One of the planes has a loudspeaker and it's my plan, if members agree, that we'll yell down, "Mr. Rosenblat." When he sticks his head out the window, then, plop, we'll let him have it! Anyway, that is my current situation with the Securities Commission in the United States. I hope I'll have the unanimous support of this House if it does come to war.
Hon. Mr. Grossman:	Except don't try to make any trips to the States now.
Mr. MacDonald:	The Minister of Consumer and Commercial Relations has offered his help already.
Hon. Mr. Clement:	We can take his Ontario licence away from him.

These Hansard excerpts were reprinted in the New York Law Journal of June 18, 1974. In response, Mr. Harold Marsh of the U.S. law firm of Nossaman, Waters, Scott, Krueger and Riordan, wrote to me that he was organizing a Lafayette Escadrille to participate with me in the water bombing of the SEC.

46 *My Poodle and Ma Bell*

As my political career was coming to its close, the ludicrous seemed to be taking precedence over the important. I had one ridiculous battle with Ma Bell.

On Wednesday May 15, the private phone which I kept in my medical office for personal conversations clunked out and I could neither phone in nor out. It was a nuisance but not a disaster because my secretary has an extension on her desk and the business phone was still working.

I must make a confession in relation to this particular phone. At the time I had it installed in 1958, there were already phones in my combination home and office in my name, my wife's name and the children's names. And so, when I put this new phone in and the telephone company asked under what name it should be listed, I foolishly said Miss Lisa Shulman.

Lisa was our pet poodle and, at the time, I did not foresee any difficulties. But over the next few years, we periodically heard from anonymous male callers asking for Miss Lisa and these tended to be of the heavy breathing type. So finally, we got Lisa an unlisted number. All then went well until the phone went out of order that Wednesday.

I immediately phoned the telephone company and asked them to come out to repair the telephone and they promised, "We will be there by 5 o'clock today." I was a little surprised when no one showed up and called the next day to inquire what had happened. The gentleman assured me they would be out by 5 o'clock that day.

On Tuesday the 21st of May, my phone was still on the blink so I phoned again. The young lady who answered this time said the repairman had been at my office at 7:30 AM Friday morning. I thought this was a little odd and pointed out to her that I had asked that they come within business hours. The young lady immediately demanded to know why, if it was a business, was it not a business phone? I explained that one to her with some difficulty and she promised that someone would be there the next day for sure.

No one arrived, so on Wednesday the 22nd I phoned again to the repair service and this time I demanded to know who I was talking to so I would know who to complain to the following day. The young lady informed me that she was not allowed to give out her name but she finally confided to me that her initials were D.M. She explained that they were very busy at the Bell Telephone Company but that someone would come the next day for sure to fix the phone.

No one came, of course, so on Thursday at 4:00 PM I phoned and I think I screamed a little at Miss D.M., whereupon she promised me faithfully that someone would be at my office by 5:00 PM. By 5:00 no one had arrived so I phoned back and asked for Miss D.M. but she had gone home. The man who answered the phone did not know the name of the night supervisor. He suggested I phone the Bell's special complaint number at 862-1020. This number was busy and remained so for the next thirty minutes.

At twenty-five to six, just as we were locking up the office, the Bell man arrived and it took him all of twenty seconds to fix the phone.

A wire had come loose where Dial-Mate had attached the automatic dialing machine which my wife had given me for my birthday. The telephone man said, "I really should not fix this – you know you are not supposed to attach non-Bell equipment to our lines." I think I was staring at him in a way that suggested imminent mayhem was about to occur for he hastily added, "I will fix it but I am going to have to report it."

At the beginning of June, a Mr. Gordon Gibson, district manager for the Bell, phoned my office and asked for an appointment. Mr. Gibson arrived the next day accompanied by Bell manager Ms. Marie Rich and they began by demanding to know if my daughter lived at home. Somewhat mystified I replied, "No, Dianne is married and lives in Huttonville."

"We do not mean Dianne," Mr. Gibson went on, "It is Lisa we are interested in."

Suddenly I understood and hastened to explain, "Oh, Lisa is not my daughter. That's our dog."

I am certain that both Mr. Gibson and Ms. Rich blanched, but after a hasty consultation, they recovered and Mr. Gibson went on, "Well, your dog has an automatic dialing service on her phone and this is in contravention of our tariffs." I asked Mr. Gibson, "But what harm is it doing? There is no risk to your equipment because the machine works only on batteries." Mr. Gibson replied, "Your dog is accessing the switching network and, unless she removes her dialing machine, we will discontinue her service."

I found it hard to take this very seriously. After all, Lisa had had her phone for fifteen years, she had always paid her bills regularly and had never caused the telephone company any difficulty. In addition, how do they expect a dog to dial? If anyone needed a dialing machine it was surely Lisa. Mr. Gibson, however, was neither amused nor placated and he and Ms. Rich left my office muttering to themselves.

I presumed that was the end of it but on July 4 I received a phone call from one C.J. Catalano, Bell's general commercial manager for Canada, who asked for an appointment to see me on a matter of urgent importance.

Mr. Catalano arrived at my office the next day to announce, "Your poodle, Lisa, is committing an illegal act by using a dialing machine that doesn't belong to the Bell. We are in the business to provide this service and we certainly do not intend to allow any competitor to have their machines attached directly to our equipment. Frankly, we cannot compete with them financially."

I suggested to Mr. Catalano that if Lisa was committing some illegal act they should charge her under the proper section of the Criminal Code. But that did not appeal to him particularly and, when I asked what law she was breaking, he was not quite certain.

"In any case" he thundered, "unless that dog removes her automatic dialing machine, we are going to cut off her phone service."

As I ushered Mr. Catalano to the door he turned and handed me his card saying, "When you write about this be sure and spell my name correctly." When I saw Catalano last, he was walking up Roncesvalles Avenue, shaking his head.

Nothing happened for three weeks until July 25 when I received a letter from Mr. Catalano saying, "Unless you notify me on or before July 29 that the device has been disconnected we will terminate telephone service." I didn't really think they were serious but, sure enough, when I arrived at the office on July 30, my poodle's phone service had been cut off.

I thought that one over for a day and then decided that there was not much point in having a rapid dialer on a disconnected phone so I reluctantly removed the machine and phoned Mr. Catalano to cry "Uncle." Within two hours the phone was reconnected and was functioning.

Now I had a problem. What was I to do with the rapid dialer which my wife had given me for my birthday? I decided to test the Bell by seeing if they treated all customers alike or just persecuted poor little dogs who cannot bark back.

I, therefore, attached the rapid dialer to the phone in my office at Queen's Park. I figured that Bell wouldn't cut off my phone without shutting down the whole Queen's Park service. But I hadn't figured on their technical abilities. Two weeks later, my Queen's Park phone extension mysteriously died, never to work again. For my remaining year as a politician, I used the pay phone down the hall.

47 *And Still More Wire Tapping*

On July 7, 1974, I received this letter:

Dear Sir:

I am writing to you to see if you might be able to help me. You are well known for exposing the wrong and getting things cleaned up.

I am a seaman. I am with the Seamen's International Union, SIU, 272 King Street, Toronto.

We had a strike and when that strike was over, myself and 16 other men were blacklisted. I went down two weeks ago to pay my union dues and was badly beaten and kicked by Mr. —. He threatened me with a baseball bat and also threatened to load up —'s shotgun.

They had me fired from my job, I am not allowed to ship out and I can't get nowhere near the hall. They have two heavies hanging around there at all times. Men have been threatened with a shotgun. Some of them have been pushed around by heavies.

I have lost my livelihood. I am out of work, can't get assistance unless the welfare comes through. At present, my hands are tied, I can't fight this alone. I will lose everything as I cannot make my payments.

I remain . . .

If this letter had been signed by one man, I would not have believed it but it carried the signature of fifteen seamen and, as a result, I began an investigation of the SIU. I discovered that:

• The union's recent agreement with the Great Lakes shippers had been overwhelmingly rejected by the seamen in an open vote in local after local. Yet, the union leadership announced when the votes were counted all across the country that the men had accepted the agreement.

• Men who objected to the agreement were blacklisted. Those who came to the union hall to complain were beaten. One of the men was beaten in the union hall in July, three days before he contacted me, in front of twenty-five other men. He was held down while a man worked him over with a baseball bat. Others were beaten on the street. One man was pulled out of a drinking parlour and attacked. One man was attacked in his home by three men who were brought down from Montreal for the job.

• I went to union headquarters in Toronto with some trepidation, armed and accompanied by a bodyguard and the union leaders there admitted keeping a shotgun handy and "tapping one man with a baseball bat to restore order."

• Companies were warned that some men were not to be hired under any circumstances or there would be a strike. These men were then refused unemployment insurance because the unions reported that work was available.

• One worker had tape-recorded conversations with a union leader in which he was told he would never work again because of his opposition to the contract.

Louis Desmarais of Montreal, chairman of Canada Steamship Lines and president of the Lake Carriers Association, told me there was nothing they could do. "The union controls who is hired and whoever controls the hiring hall controls the waterfront."

My visit to Desmarais was a Keystone Cops affair. I was by now working closely with the intelligence unit of the OPP and, when I flew to Montreal, I was accompanied by one of their officers. We were met at the airport by a unit of the Montreal urban police who fitted me with a recording device and who were then supposed to drive me to Desmarais' home in a police car disguised as a taxi. Unfortunately, the officers were not familiar with Westmount and we drove and drove until I was an hour late for my appointment. Finally, they went into a drug store to get directions. It seems that the two men assigned to the job had just arrived from Laval. Afterwards, I asked for a copy of the tape and a shamefaced officer told me, "We couldn't figure out how to make the machine work."

(I had one other very strange experience on this trip. Prior to leaving for Montreal, I had received a phone call from someone who said he was an RCMP officer. He instructed me, on my arrival in Montreal's Dorval Airport, to enter the first men's room after leaving the ramp and there to go into the second cubicle where I would find something of value. Curious, I followed the instructions and there, taped to the underside of the toilet bowl, was an envelope stuffed with about a hundred pages of transcripts of RCMP wire taps of individuals like Johnny Papalia and Paoli Violi. The transcripts of the tapes were in the original Italian with translations into both English and French. The conversations were entirely innocuous and consisted of personal "how are things" conversations interspersed with arguments over what they were going to have for supper. I could not quite figure out what to do with this find and amused myself with twitting the RCMP over the lack of importance of these conversations. The RCMP brass were not amused and demanded their return. When I refused, they threatened to raid my home – a threat they never carried through.)

Back in Toronto, I took the sworn evidence and the other affidavits I had collected to Solicitor General George Kerr and asked him to call a Royal Commission. He responded that he did not have that authority and suggested I talk to Attorney General Robert Welch. Welch wanted to know why the police just didn't lay charges. I explained that the witnesses were afraid to testify and a Royal Commission was, therefore, needed. Welch thought it over for a few days and finally refused the Commission, saying the province did not have jurisdiction over a federally chartered union.

The union leaders were certainly not worried about federal action. The OPP and the RCMP had tapes of their phone conversations in which they boasted of their close ties to the Liberal cabinet in Ottawa.

I was getting nowhere. Finally, on November 19, 1974, I made a speech in the Legislature giving all the details and concluding, "Someone in Ottawa has been paid off. I don't know who, but they boast about this at union headquarters. They don't have to worry about the federal government. They made massive contributions in the last campaign to certain key Liberals. I don't know who they are but I know that contributions were made."

Now the fat was in the fire. On November 21, 1974, Federal Labour Minister John Munro challenged me to back up my charges. He said, "I am unaware of any attempts by SIU members to bribe federal officials into ignoring union violence. Shulman is smearing an entire union and officials in the federal public service without providing any proof of his allegations." He made it quite clear there would be no federal Royal Commission. Munro finished his statement with this comment: "I did not accept nor did anyone associated with my campaign accept any contributions from the SIU in this election or any other election."

The day after Munro made his statement, I was called by someone who said he was in the police. He told me that charges of pointing a firearm, possession of an offensive weapon and common assault were being laid against two of the union leaders. He suggested that, if I were to attach a tape recorder to my phone and be ready to receive a call at 8:00 PM that evening, I would hear something of interest. What I heard was the tape of a conversation between Labour Minister Munro and Roman Gralewicz, head of the SIU. Part of it contained this gem:

Gralewicz: I want to give you a little money for your campaign. I'm going to give you $500.

Munro: Thanks a million.

Gralewicz: Well, no, it's not a million; that's for the good guys. All you so and sos get is $500.

I promptly and publicly turned the tape over to the RCMP. John Munro then admitted receiving the $500 but said he had sent the money back after the election. (It was sent back on September 3rd, 1974, several months after the election.) Federal Solicitor General Warren Allmand announced that he was investigating the matter, that he had listened to the tape and "I say there is nothing in the tape. Munro did nothing wrong in accepting the contribution."

On December 3rd, 1974, I continued the battle in the Legislature by attacking Allmand whom I suggested should not be conducting the inquiry because:
- he too had accepted a contribution from the SIU.
- the SIU had assigned a team of workers to assist him in his election.
- Allmand's official agent was the lawyer for the SIU.
- Allmand, in his role as MP, had requested the government to do more for the SIU.

I made it quite clear that none of this showed involvement in bribery or corruption on the part of either minister. What it did show was such a cosy and friendly relationship that the federal government could not be expected to act against the union. Furthermore, when the RCMP interviewed Roman Gralewicz, he boasted that he was immune because the SIU had a certain cabinet minister "in our pocket," naming a third federal minister. I was shocked at the name of this particular minister whom I had always thought of as Mister Clean and as a potential future Prime Minister. I phoned him and asked him point blank about the SIU and he replied that he was in no one's pocket. He did say, however, that he had a close personal friendship with the former president of the SIU.

The reaction to my material was violent. Gralewicz called me "a self-serving publicity seeker" and compared me to Adolph Hitler and Senator Joe McCarthy. He said that I was trying to keep in the public eye in order to peddle my books and he demanded that I be prosecuted for violation of the Protection of Privacy Act. Warren Allmand called me "the most dishonest muckraker that I have ever come up against." Scott Young in the *Globe and Mail* called me a McCarthyite, said I had smeared John Munro and demanded I be punished. And the *Montreal Star* got in the act by also comparing me to McCarthy.

Pierre Elliott Trudeau said that he had no intention of calling a public inquiry into the SIU. He suggested that the Ontario authorities had failed in their duty and that their police were incompetent. Surprisingly, George Kerr announced that he had ordered an investigation of how I received my information. But Kerr went on to say that he was demanding that the federal government conduct a probe. "The violence, intimidation and hiring hall procedures of the SIU are so out of hand that we believe only a federal inquiry can clean up the situation."

The Liberal government refused this request from Ontario. But, in response to pressure from the Tories and NDP in the House of Commons, they ordered the RCMP to investigate whether any politician had committed any illegal action in their association with the SIU. This quieted the turmoil and the following April, Solicitor General Allmand announced that the report completely absolved the politicians. He refused to make public the report but the very next day an RCMP officer told me that the report contained a sworn statement from within the SIU that three cabinet ministers had received $54,000. When I disclosed this, the embarrassed Solicitor General admitted that the report contained this allegation but that it was "completely false." He released nine pages of the thirty-seven-page report which stated that no Liberal MP had been bribed.

The next day, Federal Justice Minister Otto Lang said that an Ontario government report on the SIU contained "certain possible material" that might justify a federal investigation into the union. But, just one day later, he announced that he had decided against holding an inquiry.

No action was ever taken against the SIU. But the glare of publicity at least produced a cessation of the violence.

48 *Dog Fights*

In September 1974, I found myself, to my great surprise, in a dog fight with Tom Hughes, head of the Ontario Humane Society. Two weeks before, I had received a tip from a police officer that dog fights were being staged across Southern Ontario and he supplied me with the names and addresses of the breeders and fight promoters. With perhaps more enthusiasm than forethought, I decided that the way to stop this activity was by public exposure and I notified the twelve men involved that I was aware of their activities and would name them in the Legislature if they did not desist. I revealed their activities to the press and said I would name them if necessary.

This produced a violent reaction from Mr. Hughes: "The last thing I wanted was publicity at this time. This is the most amateurish, naïve, stupid thing Mr. Shulman could possibly have done. It will only drive the participants further underground."

Oddly enough, I had called Tom Hughes before I began my investigation. I asked for his co-operation and offered to work with him, but he had given me a flat no. I told him that I was interested only in stopping the fights but he had been anxious to have the offenders prosecuted.

No one was prosecuted. Perhaps Tom Hughes was right and I simply drove the dog fighters underground. I honestly don't know.

49 *More Asbestos*

My last major battle was over the safety of our drinking water. In December 1974, a member of the Canada-U.S. Great Lakes Research Advisory Board for the International Joint Commission sent me an unpublished report of the Board which stated that the levels of asbestos in our drinking water might produce an epidemic of cancer twenty to forty years down the road. My informant told me that the report was being kept secret for fear of alarming the public about the dangers of drinking water from the Great Lakes. On December 17, 1974, I queried Environment Minister William Newman in the House and he replied, "I don't know what report you are talking about. Metro water is safe to drink." I showed him the report and urged him to undertake a program of upgrading municipal filtration plants so as to eliminate asbestos.

The next day, Newman issued a six-page statement in which he did not dispute the facts I had presented but accused me of "unscientific" conduct in releasing the report which he said I had done only for "self-serving" purposes. The minister said he was "surprised that, of all the members of this House, a doctor of medicine would hesitate to respect the scientific ethic which dictates maximum caution in the dissemination of scientific data!" He reiterated that Ontario water was safe to drink. Newman was backed up by Professor John Brown, Chairman of the Department of Environmental Health at the University of Toronto, who said, "To attempt to alarm people without proper evidence is a public mischief. From the evidence now available I say that Morton Shulman is behaving in an irresponsible manner and creating a public mischief."

The following day, Newman followed up this broadside by saying that international researchers had concluded, as a result of three different studies on rats, that there was no evidence that swallowing asbestos caused cancer. I found Newman's statement extraordinary because the American Medical Association Journal had just published an article from a study on humans that said that the death rate from cancer of the bowel was higher in areas where the water asbestos level was high.

On January 8, 1975, U.S. researcher Sam Epstein, Professor of Environment at Case Western Reserve University in Cleveland, joined the battle issuing a statement, "There is an overwhelming scientific presumption that asbestos in the water can cause human cancer and will cause human cancer. This position is shared by virtually all the authorities in the field except those in the pay of the asbestos industry." Professor Epstein called for immediate steps to reduce asbestos in drinking water and said that to continue to drink water was a form of Russian roulette. I received further support from Dr. Irving Selikoff, international asbestos expert and director of the environmental sciences laboratory of New York's Mount Sinai School of Medicine, who released a report to the U.S. Senate proving that asbestos passes from drinking water through the bowel into human body tissues.

I obtained an estimate from the Delta Research Laboratories that it would cost $185,000 to improve asbestos removal to more than 99 per cent from the Toronto water supply. I appealed to the Legislature, "Newman may be wrong or I may be wrong. If I am wrong and you listen to me, we're going to waste some money. If Newman's wrong and you listen to him, we're going to waste a lot of lives."

Publicly the government was unmoved and minister Newman replied, "So far, no one has shown carcinogenic effects from asbestos in water." Officials in this ministry bitterly attacked me for "frightening the public." But privately the minister had been impressed by the evidence and, on January 9, 1975, he issued orders "to reduce the amount of asbestos in drinking water."

I wasn't impressed that anything effective was going to be done and I purchased a water distiller from Corning Glass. I took my still home but, when I called a technician to install it, I was told that it was illegal for a homeowner to have a still. Furthermore, the federal Excise Department said that I would be arrested if I persisted. I gave details of this stupidity to the press and there was a rapid change of heart. Mr. R.S. Dollard, regional head of the Excise Department, said, "The department's policy has been to discourage people from having stills in their homes for any purpose. However, the policy has been changed in light of the changing times."

I still use my still. Asbestos is still in Ontario's drinking water. William Newman is still a minister of the Crown. And the rate of cancer of the bowel in people drinking water from the Great Lakes is increasing.

Like so many of my fights, this one seemed to peter out with no results. But I never got really frustrated because it seemed that before one battle was over, I was up to my neck in another. There was no time for either frustration or boredom.

50 *Guns, Uranium and the Chinese*

In my last few weeks as an MPP, I got into a fight which greatly disturbed me, plus two capers which came to nothing. The fight was over the medical school at the University of Toronto.

Until 1967, the university had a quota system: 10 per cent of the places were held for women, 15 per cent for Jews, and a few places were set aside for children of doctors and for children of other alumni – the balance of the class being filled with the best qualified WASPs and Catholics. A new Dean of Medicine was appointed that year and he objected so strenuously to this system that it was changed to eliminate all favouritism by using a computer to select the students with the best marks.

The new system came into effect in 1970 and, the first year, 30 per cent of the class were landed immigrants, mostly Chinese. They were brilliant, they studied constantly and they did fantastically well on the written exams. All went well until 1974 when these students started their clinical classes and the professors discovered that many of them could not comprehend spoken English and could not communicate with the patients. They had learned English from books and could read and write it but could not understand a word. Suddenly, the medical school was faced with the terrible problem of graduating large numbers of doctors who would not understand what their patients were complaining of and who would be unable to make themselves understood by the patients.

The Medical Alumni Association, the professors and the medical profession were all upset, as were the thousands of rejected Canadian students (241 accepted out of 10,000 applicants). But no one spoke up for fear of being labelled a racist. In 1974, in the incoming class, 61 of the 240 places were given to students from other countries, many of whom could not speak a word of English.

On March 21, 1975, I decided to face the problem and raised it for the first time in the Legislature.

> I want to talk about the unthinkable for a moment. I want to talk about the students who are coming from Hong Kong and Korea and Singapore and are getting in. There is a great deal of tragedy in these cases, and I have the greatest sympathy for what they have suffered in those other countries. They come over here with their entire families' futures depending on what they do. They do nothing but study and they get incredibly good marks.
>
> The way they do that is they don't socialize. They don't go out with girls. They don't play sports. They don't do anything but work.
>
> I can understand their motivation because, when they succeed and get into medicine, they get a lucrative position which represents everything. They will be able to bring in their families from these countries and support them.
>
> I can sympathize but their problems must come secondary to ours and ours are to educate our own students first.
>
> I don't say we should cut these people out completely. We have an obligation to the rest of the world and we have to decide how big that obligation is. I think it is

not unreasonable to say we have 240 places in our class this year and we should set aside 10 per cent of those places for students from other countries. Perhaps we should set aside another ten or fifteen places for students from other provinces . . .

The minister says no. He says we mustn't do that because this is against the Human Rights Code. Well, I say – and I am agreed with by the leader of the Liberal party, by many backbenchers in the Conservative party and I know by at least some people over here; I know that I am supported by the Medical Alumni Association and I know that I am supported by the many doctors that I have had an opportunity to talk to in the last few weeks – I say that the majority of the seats in the faculty of medicine at the University of Toronto and everywhere else in this province must be kept for the students who have graduated from our high schools, who have gone through our courses of study. If their marks are lower, there are other factors that must be considered.

What do I say to the doctor who practises with me on Roncesvalles Avenue, two blocks down, who came to my office three days ago, whose son has planned all his life to take over his father's practice? Two years ago he came to the point where he could apply for medicine and was rejected. He took another year at university to perk up his marks, got them up to an A average and was rejected again last year. He is taking a fourth year at university now, getting another degree and pushing his marks up again.

He will be rejected again because he can't match up against the students who have taken their Grade 13 in another country. They come over here and repeat it again and they know it backwards, forwards and upside down.

Everyone professed to be outraged at me and I was called a racist from such varied sources as the Minister of Education and numerous student organizations. An editorial in the McMaster University paper was headed, "Shulman Stating Case for Racists." A professor of psychiatry at the University of Toronto wrote the *Star* to call me reprehensible and he was followed by numerous other civil libertarians who felt I had let them down.

I usually shrugged off attacks but I found this abuse quite painful. I had always thought of myself as a fighter for the underdog and now, suddenly, so many former supporters had turned upon me.

I think I was correct in my stand and both the government and the university came to agree with me. Initial support came from Health Minister Frank Miller and the future Minister of Labour, Bette Stephenson. Nothing was ever said publicly but the university instituted a new system of combining the computer scanning with an interview and the problem quickly disappeared.

On June 5, 1975, I brought an automatic rifle into the Legislature and scared half to death the MPPs who thought I had finally gone bonkers and was about to kill them all. It wasn't a frivolous gesture. Canada's gun laws are so lax as to be a disgrace and every year or so someone kills a few innocent people in a crazy spree.

I went to a sporting goods store in Toronto and purchased a small calibre semi-automatic rifle which I smuggled into the House under my coat. As question period began, I demanded that Attorney General John Clement tighten up on the easy sale of these weapons and suddenly produced my rifle to prove the point.

It was an amazing sight. The Tories all jumped under their desks and, as I waved the rifle toward the Liberal benches, they followed suit. The Sergeant-at-Arms jumped to his feet, hand on his sword and the Speaker ordered me to remove my weapon.

As usual, the Tories waxed indignant. The Solicitor General called me irresponsible and Energy Minister Dennis Timbrell denounced my "grandstand" play. Premier Bill Davis did see the point, however, and said that he would urge the federal government to tighten up on

gun sales. The federal government did introduce a tightened gun control bill the following year but it was diluted to impotence under pressure from the gun lobby.

The other caper had an even more serious purpose but was no more successful. On August 1, 1975, I received a phone call from an engineer at the Pickering nuclear power station complaining that there was no security at the station. A lone terrorist could easily walk in and blow up the storage room full of radioactive rods and poison the whole lake and surrounding area. My inform- ant instructed me on how to get into Pickering and, on August 4th at 8:00 AM, I entered the station through the cafeteria, put on a hard hat, and walked all the way into the spent fuel bay where the radioactive rods were stored. I left a satchel behind and walked out uneventfully, proceeding directly to Energy Minister Timbrell's office to demand that he arrange proper security for the plant. He confided to me that at that moment, there was only one guard for the entire Pickering installation.

Lawrence Woodhead, director of the Nuclear Generating Division of Hydro, issued a statement saying that Hydro did not want "military type security" because of cost and because it "is not warranted at this time."

The outcome was that Dennis Timbrell ordered that security be doubled. As a result, one extra guard was hired!

51 *Would You Like to be Ombudsman?*

I regretted the end of it all: the fights, the successes, the capers, the fun, even the defeats. But I had announced after the 1971 election that I would not run again in High Park and, in the spring of 1975, the NDP in that area chose as my successor Ed Ziemba, a local store owner. I awaited the September election and my retirement with mixed feelings.

I had played so many games with the Tories over the years that perhaps it was appropriate for them to play the last joke on me. Bill Davis invited me to visit him in his office where he asked if I would like to have a government job. He pointed out that the province was about to appoint an official Ombudsman. I swallowed the bait, burbled my enthusiasm and rushed out to prepare my plans for a storefront Ombudsman office with two secretaries, an assistant and two investigators – total annual budget $100,000 including $100 per week for myself.

Two months later, Davis appointed Arthur Maloney to the job, and Maloney wasted no time in setting up a huge bureaucracy. I couldn't help smiling the next year when I heard the Ombudsman quarrelling with the government over an extra million or two for his budget.

In June I was visiting my daughter in Brampton, Bill Davis' home riding, when a delegation of unhappy local citizens approached me to ask me to run for the NDP in that riding. I was mightily intrigued and hired a pollster to sound out my chances. To my delight, he said that I would easily beat Davis.

I made an appointment to see Stephen Lewis and offered him a proposition. I would run against Davis in Brampton and, at the very least, tie him down during the campaign. If I won, the Tories would have lost their leader but, even if I lost, they would be forced to pour workers and energy into Brampton that would otherwise be directed elsewhere across the province. In return, if the NDP were to form the government and Lewis became Premier, I wanted his public promise that he would appoint me to head the combined departments of the Solicitor General and Attorney General. (I also asked him to produce a balanced budget.)

Lewis asked for a few days to think it over and the following Monday called me back into his office to ask me, "What would be your first action as Attorney General?" I quipped, "I think I would arrest the Premier."

My joke cost me dearly for Stephen Lewis had been wavering over his decision and I had made up his mind for him. He said, "No deal." And it was all over.

My retirement from politics produced few tears. Conservatives, Liberals, and even many of my colleagues in the NDP were glad to see me go. If I received an epitaph, it was in an editorial in the Kingston *Whig-Standard*. Perhaps I can be forgiven if I reprint it – it makes me very proud.

SHULMAN: HONOURABLE GAD-FLY

Dr. Morton Shulman, New Democratic party member of the Ontario Legislature for Toronto-High Park since 1967, has announced that he is giving up his political career. His reason, "No one in office gives a damn – about inflation, the economy or the law."

The Conservative government at Queen's Park which, in many versions, has been in power since one of its founding members forged the anchor for Noah's cruise ship, will now be able to draw its daily breath free from the choking feeling Dr. Shulman so regularly induces session after session. Parallel with the triumph for Queen's Park is the profound loss to the people of Ontario.

Dr. Shulman has caused successive Conservative governments in Ontario more embarrassment than any other dozen MLAs past or present. He had a preternaturally keen nose for the special dealing which goes on behind government facades. He also happened to be financially independent. That permitted him not only to conduct elaborate private investigations but gave him enviable personal freedom of action. He was that almost unheard-of phenomenon – a rich man who happened also not to be a member of the recognized establishment; and on top of that, he was a member of the one professedly anti-establishment political party in Ontario and Canada.

From his days as Metro Coroner, when he uncovered such murky official procedures in that office that he was fired for his pains, to his single-handed exposure of certain conflict of interest figures in the government – including the then Attorney General, Dalton Bales – he slaughtered the Philistine with precision and gratifying finality.

Dr. Shulman had a fault, though. He was impetuous and sometimes failed to make a quite impregnable case. Queen's Park can muster a pretty impressive array of legal and political talent when it must and just occasionally "Morty" had to back off. He got into a mess over the Dalton Bales affair through a technical failure in a witness. Dr. Shulman offered to resign but only if there was an immediate by-election in his riding. He knew his constituents would promptly re-elect him.

The government knew it too. And, though the yells of outraged virtue from the government were strident, nobody tried seriously to swat the gad-fly once and for all.

His going from Queen's Park is a sad thing. He did care about decency in public life and administration. As he said when he made his announcement, nobody in office in Queen's Park gives a damn.

> We're sorry to see him go. Where will Ontario ever find another like him?

Post-MPP, my life has changed radically. I have abandoned politics and so have far more time for personal pursuits. I still write my column in the *Sun*, and have a weekly TV show but the energy I gave to public battles now goes to family, friends, travel and play.

I look back now over those eight hectic years with much amazement and no regrets. I made some mistakes and got clobbered for them. But, if I had "played it safe," I would not have had my successes. I would never repeat the political experience – the price in wear and tear, abuse of self and family and continual personal aggravation is just too high. But I don't regret a moment of it. I felt a sense of personal achievement that I suspect few persons ever know . . . and also, I enjoyed myself. It really was fun!